Involving CHILDREN in FAMILY SUPPORT and CHILD PROTECTION

Edited by David Shemmings
University of East Anglia, Norwich

London: The Stationery Office

© David Shemmings 1999

All rights reserved. No part of this publication may be reproduced, stored in a retrieval system, or transmitted in any form or by any means, electronic, mechanical, photocopying, recording or otherwise without the permission of the publisher.

Applications for reproduction should be made in writing to The Stationery Office Limited, St Crispins, Duke Street, Norwich NR3 1PD

The information contained in this publication is believed to be correct at the time of manufacture. Whilst care has been taken to ensure that the information is accurate, the publisher can accept no responsibility for any errors or ommissions or for changes to the details given. Every effort has been made to trace copyright holders and to obtain permission for the use of copyright material. The publishers will gladly receive any information enabling them to rectify any errors or omissions in subsequent editions.

David Shemmings has asserted his moral rights under the Copyright, Designs and Patents Act 1988, to be identified as the author of this work.

A Library of Congress CIP catalogue record has been applied for.

First published 1999

ISBN 0 11 322117 7

Published by The Stationery Office and available from:

The Publications Centre
(mail, telephone and fax orders only)
PO Box 276, London SW8 5DT
Telephone 0870 600 5522
Fax orders 0870 600 5533

The Stationery Office Bookshops
123 Kingsway, London WC2B 6PQ
0171 242 6393 Fax 0171 242 6394
68–69 Bull Street, Birmingham B4 6AD
0121 236 9696 Fax 0121 236 9699
33 Wine Street, Bristol BS1 2BQ
0117 926 4306 Fax 0117 929 4515
9–21 Princess Street, Manchester M60 8AS
0161 834 7201 Fax 0161 833 0634
16 Arthur Street, Belfast BT1 4GD
01232 238451 Fax 01232 235401
The Stationery Office Oriel Bookshop
18–19 High Street, Cardiff CF1 2BZ
01222 395548 Fax 01222 384347
71 Lothian Road, Edinburgh EH3 9AZ
0131 228 4181 Fax 0131 622 7017

The Stationery Office's Accredited Agents
(see Yellow Pages)

and through good booksellers

Printed in the United Kingdom by Albert Gait, Grimsby.
J72492 C20 05/99 9385 9862

CONTENTS

	PAGE
Introduction – **David Shemmings**	iii
1. Versions of childhood – **Dr Liz Trinder**	1
2. Children's views of their involvement – **Ian Butler** and **Dr Howard Williamson**	7
3. Children's rights – **David Hodgson**	15
4. Planning and reviewing with children in substitute care – **Yvonne Shemmings**	23
5. Research into children's involvement in child protection conferences – **David Shemmings**	29
6. Children's perspectives on attending statutory reviews – **Steve Walker**	35
7. Attachment theory – **Professor David Howe**	43
8. Making sense of separation and loss: the child's experience – **Gillian Schofield**	51
9. Defences and adaptive responses – **Dr Judith Trowell**	59
10. Emotional and cognitive development – **Diana Hinings**	63
11. Communicating with children and ascertaining their wishes and feelings – **Marian Brandon**	69
12. Children with communication difficulties – **Janet Lees**	77
13. The importance of relationships – **David Shemmings**	85
14. Child advocacy – **Nicky Scutt**	93
15. User groups – **Dee Lynes, Jim Goddard,** and **Stewart Betts**	99
16. Preparing children for involvement in decision-making – **Alison Corner, Catherine Rushforth** and **David Shemmings**	105
17. Professional supporters and children's involvement – **Alison Corner**	111
18. Using professional judgement – **Catherine Kenney**	117
Authors' CVs	126
Acknowledgements	127

INTRODUCTION
David Shemmings

This book is one of three components of a Department of Health initiative aimed at increasing the involvement of children in family support and child protection processes. The second element consists of a training pack, *In On The Act* (Shemmings 1998), for relevant professionals in these areas of child welfare. The third part of the project is a resource pack, *Turning Points*, published in 1998 by the National Society for the Prevention of Cruelty to Children (NSPCC) and Chailey Heritage.

One might wonder what all the fuss is about. Children today are involved in areas of decision-making unthinkable a few years ago: who could have predicted that infants would have advertising aimed directly at them, as many people feel we are witnessing in the United Kingdom; similarly, quite young children are involved in decisions about medical interventions nowadays, including whether or not to continue treatment during the later stages of terminal illness. Therefore, if many of the markers that distinguish adults from children are disappearing in other aspects of young people's lives, then why not involve them more in decisions about child welfare and protection?

For most professionals, the real question here, however, is not *whether* we involve children in such decisions but *how* we do so. How exactly does a social worker ask a 5-year-old girl whether she wants to remain in the care of her mother who, whilst regularly telling her daughter that she loves her, nevertheless leaves her on her own when depressed and suicidal? How does a foster carer make sense of the expressed wishes of a 10-year-old boy who, on the Monday morning following a visit to his father in prison over the weekend, says he wants to live with his dad when he comes out on Wednesday but by Friday has changed his mind? How does a teacher respond to a 14-year-old who says 'I'd rather stay with my dad than go into care, even though he does things to me that he shouldn't.'?

Asking children to express their wishes and feelings is a relatively straightforward task. Provided that the practitioner is aware of a few basic techniques, finding out children's preferences is not that difficult even with children at quite young ages. The problem for the worker is how to *make sense of the answers*. It is the same as in the area of assessment: virtually anyone can gather information; the complex task is that of evaluating and weighing it all up. Furthermore, asking a child how she or he feels about something is a difficult question to answer: for example, how do *you* feel, right now? If we are honest, the answer often is simply 'cold' or 'hungry' – but this is not really what social workers and others want children to say. Now imagine that you are asked, 'How do you feel about where you want to live, and with whom, over the next ten years or so?' or 'How do you feel about your parents/your partner/your brother/your sister?' Just to complicate the picture even more, it is now thought that finding out how the child *thinks* – about themselves, and their main relationships, but more importantly, how these two aspects of the child's inner world interrelate – is as crucial, if not more so, than finding out about their feelings (Brandon, Schofield and Trinder 1998).

Because of the paucity of training materials to help practitioners develop the skills needed to involve young people more effectively, especially when they are thought to be at risk, it is no surprise to find that professionals sometimes flounder when faced with the job of finding out children's thoughts, wishes, and feelings. Practitioners can become very polarised in their attitudes, either by stressing the rights of the young person to be an active participant in all decision-making processes or by rescuing the child from any involvement in case it could cause harm. But this 'Rights' versus 'Rescue' polarisation, like all simple, binary, 'either/or' categorisations, overlooks or ignores completely the complex nature of children's involvement in family support and child protection.

Two examples will illustrate the 'Rights versus Rescue' polarisation. The first concerns a 12-year-old boy who, when asked by one of the professionals what he thought about going to a recent child protection conference, said 'Looking back, I'm glad I went; but I bet you thought I shouldn't have gone, don't you?' 'No,' said the professional, 'but why do you say that?' The boy replied, quite assertively:

> Because you saw me crying in the meeting, when they talked about what my dad did to me. You're right. I was upset, because I didn't know they would say things like that with him there; but if I had known they were going to do this I'd have been OK. I was angry with [my social worker] for not preparing me properly. All he did was tell me where the meeting was and who would be there. But, when I cried in the middle of the meeting, I could feel everyone thinking that I shouldn't be there. But that's so patronising. Why can't you lot understand that *I was there when he abused me, so why shouldn't I be there when you talk about it?* [my italics]

The second example refers to a 13-year-old girl who, when asked what she remembered about going to a child protection conference, said: 'I didn't agree with them offering my mum a cup of coffee.' 'Why is that?' asked an adult known to the child. Her answer was angrily expressed:

> Because she abuses me. I thought they were all going to tell her to stop hitting me all the time; but no, not only do they not tell her off, they're all nice to her and she gets offered a cup of coffee.

The worrying aspects in both these examples could, of course, have been minimised or even overcome completely if the young people had been prepared better. The negative consequences could have been transformed into positive events; self-efficacy – knowing that what we do can, and does, make a difference – could so easily have replaced feelings of powerlessness, thus strengthening the child's self-concept and experience of self-worth. This in turn enhances resilience (Fonagy *et al* 1994) in children and young people.

Professionals who tend towards the 'Rights' end of the spectrum will argue that the first example supports their position by highlighting the consequences when adults think they know what is best for children, while those veering towards the 'Rescue' end of the continuum will cite the second example as proof that attending a meeting can harm children. This book argues that, in both examples, more information is needed in order to work out, in partnership with young people, how best to involve them in decision-making. The book provides readers with much of this information. By including chapters from a psychosocial tradition together with those of a more civil-libertarian perspective, the book aims to overcome this tendency to polarise attitudes. Hence, the reader will see that a knowledge of child advocacy, for example, is complemented by an understanding of attachment theory, provided that the nature and extent

Introduction

of the child's level of resilience is taken into account.

In the following 18 chapters, readers are presented with contemporary research findings outlined in an easily digestible way for busy practitioners and managers. The first 6 introduce key topics about the involvement of children in decision-making. Liz Trinder begins by discussing 'childhood' as a social construction. Ian Butler and Howard Williamson follow by reflecting what young people themselves have had to say about being involved in decision-making. In Chapter 3, David Hodgson explores the concept of children's rights, as well as some of the tensions and dilemmas, when it is applied to child welfare. Chapters 4, 5 and 6 summarise practice and research in three key areas of children's involvement: Yvonne Shemmings considers how children who experience substitute care can be more involved in planning and review processes; I go on to summarise research about their involvement in child protection conferences; and Steve Walker then returns to the theme of substitute care by considering the perspectives of children who have actually attended statutory child care reviews.

The next five chapters consider children's involvement from a more psychosocial perspective. In Chapter 7, David Howe outlines the main reasons why professionals seeking to involve young people in decision-making need to understand attachment theory. Next, Gillian Schofield explains how an awareness of separation and loss is important when working with children. Judith Trowell then considers how children's defences and adaptive responses can help professionals interpret children's reactions. In Chapter 10, Diana Hinings explores how 'normal' emotional and cognitive development in young people can inform practitioners' assessments of 'age appropriateness'. Marian Brandon follows this by outlining ways in which professionals can improve their communication skills with children.

The last seven chapters explore related aspects of children's involvement. Janet Lees, in Chapter 12, discusses how children with communication difficulties can end up even more marginalised if those working with them are not aware of how to understand their experiences. Next, I consider the nature of the relationship between workers and young people; not surprisingly, trust, openness and the ability to show genuine concern and respect remain at the centre. In Chapter 14, Nicky Scutt discusses findings from her research into the use of child advocacy and then, in a similar vein, Dee Lynes, Jim Goddard and Stewart Betts explore how user groups can help young people in practical ways. The subject of preparing children to take a more active part in decision-making processes, as well as briefing them afterwards, is considered a topic in its own right; hence, Chapter 16, by Alison Corner, Catherine Rushforth and myself, suggest practical approaches to prevent children being caught off-guard. In Chapter 17, Alison Corner suggests different ways in which professionals can be better supported, in what is clearly a complex and difficult aspect of direct work with children.

In the final chapter, which tackles the use of professional judgement, Catherine Kenny describes a situation in which a 9-year-old boy expresses seven different views, in as many weeks, about who he wants to live with. Given his circumstances, each of his expressed wishes and feelings are perfectly genuine and logically consistent. This final chapter captures perfectly the dilemmas facing professionals when trying to involve children in decisions about family support and child protection. How can the tension be resolved: how do professionals avoid the trap of the 'Rights versus Rescue' polarisation? It is argued, both in this book and in the training pack *In On The Act*, that the best way to proceed is for practitioners to appreciate that the only sensible answer to the question 'Should children be involved in family support and child protection decisions?' is 'It depends . . . . ' What the following chapters help readers to assess, for each child with whom they come into contact, is more precisely what 'it depends' upon.

References

Brandon, M., Schofield, G. and Trinder, L. (1998) *Social Work with Children*. London: Macmillan.

Fonagy, P., Steele, M., Steele, H., Higgitt, A. and Mayer, L. S. (1994) 'The Emmanuel Miller Memorial Lecture 1992. The theory and practice of resilience', *Journal of Child Psychology and Psychiatry*, vol. 35, no. 2., pp. 231–58.

National Society for the Prevention of Cruelty to Children/Chailey Heritage (1998) *Turning Points: A Resource Pack for Communicating with Children*. London: NSPCC.

Shemmings, D. (1998) *In On The Act: Involving Children in Family Support and Child Protection – A Training Pack for Professionals*. Norwich: University of East Anglia.

CHAPTER 1

VERSIONS OF CHILDHOOD
Liz Trinder

What is a child? What is childhood? These seem big questions, but with straightforward answers. Most of us would say that we know quite a lot about children. We have all been children, some of us have had children, and some of us have worked with children. We all know what we mean when we call other people's behaviour 'childish'. A respected science of child psychology has emerged to map out the developmental stages on the route from infancy to adulthood.

But things are not so simple. Where and when we live fundamentally shapes how we think about and treat children and childhood. What it means to be a child is socially constructed and each society constructs it differently; there is nothing fixed or natural about childhood. Instead, each society, at different periods, creates its own version, or versions, of childhood. Each society, for example, has different ideas and rules about how long childhood lasts. Some societies have thought about how best to involve children in decision-making, others have pondered over whether or not children should be involved in decisions concerning them, and in some societies the question of child involvement would never even be considered.

To date, versions of childhood have oscillated, based on an understanding of children as either different from adults or as broadly similar to adults. In the first version childhood is seen as qualitatively different from adulthood. Children are held to be less capable and more vulnerable than adults and hence require special protection and to have decisions made for them. In the second version the differences between adults and children are seen to be less pronounced, with the implication that children should be treated similarly to adults. Participation in decision-making therefore becomes more important.

My aim in this chapter is to identify some of these different versions of childhood. I also look at how different versions of childhood shape both child care policy and practice. I finish by recommending that practitioners should avoid basing practice on just one side of the similarity/difference dichotomy.

Childhood in time: time for childhood?

The emergence of the modern child: difference and dependency

Recent debates about childhood were sparked by the publication in 1962 of *Centuries of Childhood,* the highly-influential book by Philippe Ariès. His central argument was that it is a comparatively recent innovation or achievement to treat children as different from adults. Ariès interpreted paintings and literature to argue that there was no separate concept of childhood in the Middle Ages. Instead, children over the age of seven simply merged into adult society. Only during the 16th and 17th centuries, Ariès argued, did the introduction of education help to usher in a separate stage of 'childhood' in the West.

Ariès's analysis has since been rebutted, but there are continuing attempts to track the development of ideas about childhood. One recent interpretation (Cunningham 1995) argues that there was a significant change in ideas about childhood, but not until the early 19th century. Cunningham argues that over the preceding century a romantic view of childhood had developed, portraying childhood as a period of innocence, of protection and of dependency, separate from the adult world. During the 19th century private philanthropists, and then the state, acted to extend this middle-class romantic view of childhood to working-class children. Such children, working in factories or fields, were seen as being denied a childhood. Children left the workplace and entered full-time schooling. Children stopped being an economic asset to their families as the right not to work was enshrined in law; gradually, they became simply an emotional asset to their parents, consumers rather than producers. A range of professions – child psychiatrists, psychologists, social workers, health visitors – emerged to advise families, but particularly mothers, on how to bring up their children according to the new norms as the state and society assumed a new responsibility for its youngest members.

Child care policy has been closely tied to different versions of childhood. Lorraine Fox Harding (1991) identified a range of perspectives underpinning British child care policy over the last hundred years. Each of these perspectives is based on different models, or constructions, of childhood and two of them are associated with this era:

- *Laissez-faire and patriarchy.* In this perspective, the family should be left to sort out its own affairs, with external (state) intervention in family life kept to a minimum. Internal family decisions about child rearing and so on are the responsibility of the family's most powerful members: the parents, especially the father. Children are subsumed, almost rendered invisible, within the family – almost 'non-persons' and distinct from autonomous adults.
- *State paternalism and child protection.* In contrast, this perspective is predicated on extensive state intervention in the family to protect children from poor parental care (as defined by professionals). Again, childhood is seen as a distinct and vulnerable stage of the life-cycle, requiring adult protection and adult decision-making. But instead of being protected by their parents within the family, children are seen as having potentially different and conflicting interests from their parents, from whom they may well need protection. As in the *laissez-faire* perspective, children are seen as having limited capacity for self-determination but now greater emphasis is placed on professionals, rather than just parents, as the adult decision-makers.

Over the course of the 19th and 20th centuries the ideal Western childhood became one where children and adults were seen as having separate natures, playing separate roles in separate spheres of activity. The only major debate was which adult decision-maker – the parent or the professional – should guide the child. David Archard (1993) summarises this point:

> In sum, the modern child is an innocent incompetent who is not but must become the adult. The 'must' conveys both the necessity of human development and the ideal character of maturity. In our culture this outlook determines the proper place of the child as one who cannot enjoy the rights and responsibilities of the adult.

But this is not a universal version of childhood. In the West the dominant version renders the child economically inactive and dependent upon adults; but in other parts of the world, particularly in developing countries, children may still take on a crucial role as producers as well as consumers and an equivalent emphasis is placed upon their responsibilities and duties to their families.

From object of concern to speaking subject

During the 19th and early 20th century we have seen that there was a broad, if incomplete, shift in the West, from Fox Harding's *laissez-faire* perspective to state *paternalism* with an accompanying reconceptualisation of childhood. Over the last two decades we have experienced another major transition. The ascendancy of the Welfare State and collectivism, established after the Second World War, has been halted by an incoming tide of liberalism and individualism. The focus shifted from collective needs and collective responses to the rights of individuals to define and defend their own interests. We now place greater emphasis on individual rights as consumers or customers and much less on the state, communities or even families to support us. Consumer choice, partnership and empowerment enable individuals to be 'freed' to make their own decisions – less often now by communities or collectives.

This broad shift has influenced almost every aspect of social and public life, primarily for adults but now extending also to children. Against this background we can understand the emergence of two newer child care perspectives identified by Fox Harding: 'Parents' Rights' and 'Children's Rights':

- *Modern defence of the birth family and parents' rights.* Like the *laissez-faire* perspective, the parents' rights perspective values the integrity of the family and opposes extensive state interference in family matters. Unlike Fox Harding's first perspective, emphasis is placed on the potentially supportive role of the state in providing services to support parents in their role. The focus is on the family unit as a whole rather than disaggregating it into its constituent parts. Reclaiming decision-making for parents from professionals assumes a much greater significance than the autonomy of the child.
- *Children's rights and children's liberation.* This perspective presents a contrasting construction of childhood. Here the emphasis is on the rationality, competence and strength of children and 'autonomy' is placed alongside 'rights to protection'; children become independent actors, with separate interests within the family. Children cannot and should not rely on their parents to act in their best interests. They must speak and act for themselves.

The Children Act 1989 – a charter for children's rights?

Some 40 years ago the idea that children had rights to have a say in decisions about them would probably have seemed bizarre to those interested in protecting them. Over the last two decades, as part of the shift identified above, policy-makers have to some extent moved towards the view of the child as 'a person and not an object of concern' (Lord Justice Butler-Sloss 1988). This has found some legislative expression in the Children Act 1989, with requirements (among others) to ascertain children's wishes and feelings on a range of matters, and to advise them of their rights to refuse medical examinations, rights to representation in public law, and rights to initiate their own court applications.

We must not get carried away though with the idea that current legislation or policy constructs children as separate, autonomous decision-makers, much like adults. What is apparent is that the Children Act contains traces of all four of Fox Harding's perspectives, but with the version of childhood based on children's rights to autonomy probably the weakest. The Act continues with a version of childhood based on vulnerability and dependency at the same time as tentatively introducing the child as a separate individual with her or his own ideas and subjectivity. Besides there being a tension between the autonomous child and the vulnerable child, the Children Act also finds itself placed between the autonomy of the child and the autonomy (or privacy) of the family.

These tensions are worked out in different ways in different areas of child care policy, depending on the subject matter. There is no consistent version of childhood. Although the version of childhood based on dependency dominates (that is, welfare is always paramount), precisely how this is worked out varies according to the issue at stake. For 'children of divorce' the emphasis is clearly on family autonomy. The principle of minimum intervention means that decisions about contact or residence are made by parents, and it is entirely up to them if and how they consult children (an example of the *laissez-faire* perspective). Only if parents disagree does the 1989 Act formally recognise children's autonomy with a requirement that children's wishes and feelings be ascertained. In contrast, the 1989 Act and accompanying Regulations pay far greater attention to the participation of all children who are being looked after.

Practice

If policy contains contradictory constructions of childhood, then so inevitably does practice. As part of a small research project, I interviewed four court welfare teams whose role included ascertaining children's wishes and feelings. I found that practice was based on, or reflected, two different versions of childhood.

Two teams that worked within a systemic perspective had much in common with Fox Harding's 'Parents' Rights' perspective. They emphasised working with parents to enhance parental decision-making, and largely equated children's interests with those of their parents. Children were seen as vulnerable rather than autonomous and children's involvement in the decision-making process was seen as burdensome and threatening. Practice was therefore based on ascertaining wishes and feelings indirectly, through parents or in 'family meetings', or by using very indirect questioning of children, focusing on 'feelings' rather than 'wishes'.

The other two teams worked in a style more akin to Fox Harding's state 'Paternalist' perspective. Again, children were seen as vulnerable, but here the source of damage was the impact of the parental divorce or separation rather than the child's participation in the decision-making process. Children's interests were perceived as potentially distinct from their parents, thereby opening up a space for professional support, intervention and assessment. Children were almost always seen directly, for a longer period, and were asked directly whether they had a view and if they wanted to share it. This more significant role was mediated by an equivalent emphasis on their childlike (that is, unreliable) status as witnesses or decision-makers. Indeed, too much emphasis on children's opinions could allow children too much power. Ascertaining wishes and feelings was therefore only partly about expressing views; it seemed more about enabling a welfare professional to make the best possible assessment of the child's needs.

These two very different social work practitioner versions of childhood can be further contrasted with the versions presented by some children's rights commentators (for example, Timms 1995). Rather than immature and incompetent objects of concern, Timms says that children become independent 'speaking subjects' whose interests are independent of and possibly in conflict with those of their parents. There is a strong presumption of children's competence to participate in decision-making, or at least to formulate their own independent views. Furthermore, Timms argues, it is harmful to children to ignore these views and it is beneficial to children to participate in decision-making. The solution to the damage caused to children by divorce comes from an articulation of the child's interests and preferred solutions, preferably through independent representation.

The right(s) approach to practice?

The case so far is that there is no natural 'essence' of childhood; our ideas about childhood are historically and culturally specific. This has not stopped people claiming to know the 'truth' about childhood. Discussions of childhood have been riddled with debates about whether children are really similar to or different from adults. The court welfare officers mentioned earlier had become wedded to a particular model of childhood, and their practice confined children within these roles. Research on children's attendance at child protection conferences similarly identified an entirely for, or entirely against, polarity amongst practitioners (Shemmings 1996).

I argue that practitioners should avoid making a forced choice between versions of childhood based on similarity or difference, liberation or paternalism, or participation or protection. This acts simply to impose a false unity on the category of 'child'. It does little justice to the structural differences within the category of 'child', including differences by gender, ethnicity, age and disability. Nor does the assumption of a single childhood recognise more individualised differences between children. For example, some Asian or orthodox Jewish children may experience difficulties in expressing their own opinions due to cultural expectations that children respect adults' decisions. But even here we are in danger of generalising about a category. 'Cultural' expectations are themselves fluid and differentiated by class and so on, let alone by the response of individual children. Some children in child protection or family support may simply want to hear information about what is going on, while others may want to be more involved and others not involved at all. In each case the choice will be based on a range of different factors and circumstances unique to that child in that context.

Additionally, the versions of childhood we have been talking about have been created by adults for children. This is a little ironic when we are talking about children's participation and involvement. Whilst we need to recognise the power adults have in defining childhood, we must recognise that children do have the power to act. Children are not simply passive objects but, even though operating from a weaker position, they act and react in response to adults as well as with other children, as research undertaken from a child's perspective indicates (for example, Fine and Sandstrom 1988).

The problem is that children do not always see the issues in the same way as adults. For example, Butler and Williamson (1994) quote a 12-year-old girl whose parents had divorced: 'I was so scared 'cos I thought I had to speak to the judge about who I wanted to live with – I didn't want to hurt anyone.'

For this girl the debate was not about being rational and competent, or emotional and incompetent. She had been involved in her own decision-making process but in this case by making a decision that the best thing for her was to keep silent rather than to participate in adult-defined processes. She had become a rational non-participant.

Conclusion

Many different versions of childhood exist. For practitioners it is essential to bear in mind that there is nothing 'natural' or 'fixed' about how we see children. Indeed, how we see children is very much influenced by the time and place we live in, and practitioners are not immune from this. I would argue that practitioners need to be as reflective as possible in identifying how their own practice constructs children. Which versions of childhood are implicit in practice? Are they flexible enough to allow children to be different things at different times? Do they allow children to define both themselves and their degree of participation?

References

Archard, D. (1993) *Children: Rights and Childhood*. London: Routledge, p. 41.

Ariès, P. (1962) *Centuries of Childhood*. London: Jonathan Cape.

Butler, I. and Williamson, H. (1994) *Children Speak: Children, Trauma and Social Work*. London: NSPCC/Longman, p. 57.

Butler-Sloss, E. (1998) *The Report of the Inquiry into Child Abuse in Cleveland*. London: HMSO.

Cunningham, H. (1995) *Children and Childhood in Western Society since 1500*. London: Longman.

Fine, G. and Sandstrom, K. (1988) *Knowing Children – Participant Observation with Children*. Newbury Park: Sage.

Fox Harding, L. (1991) *Perspectives in Child Care Policy*. London: Longman.

Shemmings, D. (1996) *Involving Children in Child Protection Conferences,* Social Work Monographs, No. 152. Norwich: University of East Anglia.

Timms, J. (1995) *Children's Representation: A Practitioner's Guide*. London: Sweet & Maxwell.

CHAPTER 2

CHILDREN'S VIEWS OF THEIR INVOLVEMENT
Ian Butler and Howard Williamson

It has become popular to talk about the way that adults invent and re-invent childhood. We have argued ourselves (Butler and Williamson 1994) that contemporary accounts of childhood constitute a deficit model, whereby children are defined primarily on the basis of their dependence in order to satisfy the unmet needs of adults.

Childhood is widely conceived of as a state of incompetence relative to adulthood. To be a child is to be 'not-yet-an-adult' nor to possess the intellectual, emotional and physical capacities to act autonomously. Adulthood is the desirable end-point of childhood and each successive stage in the development of the 'not-yet-an-adult' is not simply a quantitative advance but a qualitative improvement upon that which went before, until 'success' is achieved in adulthood. By this reading, adulthood is a settled state of being and childhood merely a process towards that end. This process is driven by a fury of evolutionary, biological and hormonal imperatives until the advent of the staid, 'middle-aged individual of modest, moderate and settled needs'.

One cannot doubt the fact of human growth and development (although the several facts are arguable) but we do draw attention to the unnecessary but pervasive assumption that childhood is not simply quantitatively and qualitatively different from adulthood (which is simply to state the obvious) but more damagingly that it is also *by its very nature less than adulthood*. It is not simply a matter of relative competence but also a matter of the cultural presumption of the subordinate status of childhood and the relative powerlessness of children with which we are concerned.

If children are generally and necessarily viewed as incompetent, inferior, yet fully understood by adults, then it is no surprise that children are abused; nor is it a surprise that they do not feature as subjects or significant actors, to any large extent, in many child protection procedures (Butler and Williamson 1996).

How, then, might a model of child protection look that had the active and purposeful involvement of children as its central goal and that reflected children's own experience and their capacity to determine the kind of help they want? What do young people themselves have to say about the nature of abuse and how they want to be helped?

Children's experience of harm

This chapter is based on the findings of a study of 200 children and young people aged between 6 and 17 and reported in depth elsewhere (Butler and Williamson 1994). Not surprisingly, given that we drew our sample from a wide range of young people, the range of harmful experiences reported to us was equally wide. What is perhaps more important is that the true meaning of an event for the child is not always the obvious one.

Even those circumstances that would register on any official continuum of abuse as extraordinarily traumatic and serious often contained meanings for the child that might not have been obvious to the casual observer. A girl of 17 who, as a 9-year-old, had experienced the murder of her mother by her father, reported the real trauma to be the lack of information and explanation available at the time:

> I never saw my mum in hospital after my dad attacked her. I didn't go to the funeral. I don't even know now where her grave is. Nobody told me anything, probably because they thought I was too young. But nobody even tried. And I can't ask now 'cos all the staff who were here then have moved on. But that was actually worse than my mum actually dying.

Even in less dramatic, but no less traumatic, situations, lack of information about the most momentous events in one's life can be an additional source of pain. The degree and duration of suffering is often greater than an adult imagines and may also be obscured by an adult belief that children 'will get over it'. Long after the abuse stops, the hurt can continue:

> I still have nightmares. Something happened to me when I was six. It was a friend of the family who used to babysit for us. My mum says not to worry, 'He won't come back.' But I still worry. In my dreams, he still comes back. (girl, 11)

Childrens' and adults' sense of what hurts can be different. Children experience other forms of adult behaviour as intensely hurtful, particularly familial arguments and domestic violence:

> I can hear my parents arguing when I'm lying in bed at night. Sometimes they're arguing about me. I can't sleep and I can't stop worrying. Quite often I'm afraid to go down in the morning. (girl, 14)

Although some adults would find it difficult to acknowledge their own arguments or their violence directed to each other as actually or potentially harmful or abusive, they can certainly hurt children.

But our study revealed that it was the routine catalogue of harm suffered by children at the hands of other children that most readily challenges adult conceptions of what constitutes abuse. Bullying, for example, enters and damages the lives of many children: 'The bullying at school can be really nasty. Sometimes, just before break time, I start to shake in class because I'm so scared about going outside.' (girl, 13) And:

> The worst thing is at school when you go out into the playground. The older kids come over and take your bag off you and chuck it around, or nick your hat and won't let you have it back. You get really upset, 'cos they're all laughing at you and you look stupid in front of your mates. (boy, 12)

> Because I'm quite good at school, I get picked on by the other girls who call me a
> 'snob' and poke and push me around. Sometimes I don't really care, but I must admit
> I do find it hard to fit in and that gets to me sometimes. (girl, 14)

The awful thing about such experiences according to the children and young people themselves was the thought that if you were to admit your terror then it would almost inevitably make things worse. You had to put up with it until the bullies moved on to someone else. Name-calling was far more prevalent and almost always regarded as just as traumatic as physical bullying. No one was entirely safe. It would be easy to underestimate the effect of even the most familiar of taunts:

> What gets to me most is being called 'four eyes'. I hate it, really hate it. I can't help
> it if I have to wear glasses. Sometimes I just want to take them off, even if I can't see
> without them. Maybe it's better not to see than to be called names all the time.
> (boy, 11)

Name-calling *does* hurt. It might not hurt an adult to the same degree (possibly) and the hurt is not as serious as the potential hurt caused by other forms of abuse towards children. However, to deny the pain it can cause in the face of what children and young people actually say is to demean children, disregard the validity of *their* accounts, and thereby perpetuate the communication gap that exists between children and adults.

Talking to the wall

Our study dealt at some length with the fact that many young people had already lost faith in adults' capacity to help them deal with their problems, to the degree that they had already entirely given up on them. Many children said that if they had a problem they would talk to no one other than their friends. Some of the reasons given by these children, based on their experiences of adults' reactions, were very widely shared. For example, it is generally believed by the children to whom we talked that adults are insensitive and lack real interest. The children who spoke to us could find no reason to discriminate between the lack of understanding displayed by what we called 'adult professionals' – for example, social workers, teachers, doctors, etc. – and 'professional adults' who were just full-time 'grown ups' (for example, parents).

> About social workers:

> They do one good thing for you and two things bad. You don't know where you
> stand. They go on about knowing what's best for you, but it's all out of books. How
> can they know your 'best interests' when they don't even know you? (girl, 14)

And, parents:

> Parents ignore you. They don't show any interest in you and then they blame you
> when things go wrong. (girl, 12)

The direct consequence of a lack of basic sensitivity or interest can be the imposition by adults of their own views. About parents, again:

> I had this fight at school and got sent home. It was the first time I'd ever had a fight and I was really upset. Dad wasn't bothered at first – he said 'Talk to mum.' Then he came in and said 'Did you win?'. . . . Adults don't understand kids' reasons, they don't hear their explanations – kids don't *win*. It's bad for both of you, but somehow you both end up fighting at the time. He's my mate. But I couldn't get a word in edgeways. My dad only wanted to know bits of the story – the bits he'd understand. He's stubborn. He didn't want to listen. And when he'd heard what *he* wanted to hear, he changed the subject. He didn't want to listen to what *I* wanted to say. (boy, 13)

Often, misunderstanding was closely followed by other inappropriate reactions. Adults can trivialise what is bothering children: 'People treat you as a joke. They don't take you seriously.' (boy, 13)

For other young people who spoke to us, the pendulum was perceived to swing suddenly from an attitude that trivialised experiences and concerns (epitomised by the expression 'Why don't you grow up?') to one that *overreacted* and adopted an overprotective and disempowering stance:

> If you tell your teacher or your parents you are getting picked on by other kids, they go in head-first and that makes things worse. When I told my dad I was being bullied, he came steaming down to the school and the teacher had a go at these kids. But they just picked on me worse 'cos they thought it was a laugh that I'd had to tell my dad. (boy, 13)

Those children we spoke to felt that the worst form of overreaction by adults is one that, in essence, 'blames the victim':

> Me and my friends always used to hang around in the park. One day there was this man there. He wasn't doing anything but he spooked me. He was there every day for about a week. So I told my mum. I got grounded for a month! It was like it was my fault. I wish I hadn't told her now. (girl, 14)

The greatest source of doubt concerning the capacity of adults to help children arose from young people's fears over possible breaches of confidentiality. A widely held belief amongst children and young people is that professionals have an enormous capacity for 'gossip' or 'blabbing':

> Sometimes social workers tell you personal things about themselves. I think they're trying to get you to trust them. But are they true? How do you know? And then they say things like 'Can you keep a secret?' and you think this is because they want you to tell them your secrets. If they're telling me secrets, they'll probably tell mine to somebody else. They're loudmouths. (girl, 11)

Finally, an ironic commentary on the issue of confidentiality was provided by young people themselves. The following exchange took place in a group interview with teenage girls:

I'd talk to Miss _____ [teacher]. She's got her head screwed on. She's caring and she'd be confidential about it.
    And she's got her own problems which she told in confidence to some of the students in the sixth form.
    Yeah, and THEY told the whole school!

Seeking help

Children and young people gave the following three reasons for approaching adults or peers to talk about their problems:

- to unload;
- to elicit ideas and possible choices for action;
- to catalyse action by others.

In our experience, young people say that they are only too aware that, ultimately, it is *they* who are most likely to bring about the resolution to their problems. Thus the first two reasons are by far the most important ones to children and young people themselves. Young people do not seek or expect action by others *unless they ask for it*. Broadly, they seek to *unload* problems on friends and seek *advice, information and guidance* from adults. Younger children are more likely to believe and hope that others can 'sort things out' on their behalf, but even the 8-to 9-year-old children we interviewed still felt that they had to take the initiative on those matters that concerned them most. As we have noted elsewhere (Butler and Williamson 1994):

The dilemma for children and young people, as they see it, is that once they convey something to adults, the power to determine what should then be done is – too often – taken out of their hands.

So what are children looking for in the help that adults can offer?

Listening to the child

Young people want individualised attention and careful listening, without adults trivialising or being dismissive of the issues raised: 'A good listener. Someone who doesn't immediately get back at you with "Oh, you're tired, you'll be all right tomorrow" – that's not listening.' (girl, 11)

Regret at being prevented from being the author of their own biography was echoed by many children and young people who looked for a non-judgmental and non-directive response from adults: 'I want my own choices – otherwise my life might be ruined by someone else's mistakes.' (girl, 12) And:

Instead of saying 'You have to do this,' say 'Why don't you try this and if you don't like it, don't bother.' People who look at things from your point of view, who take time to find out what *you're* thinking is best for you. (boy, 14)

As a 14-year-old girl put it: 'I think everybody needs advice from time to time but not from people who talk down to you.' She believed that people should give you choices: 'This is what I'd do, but it's up to you.'

Children recognise early that life is the art of the possible and value honesty and 'straight talking' in the adults around them. About a teacher: 'She's prepared to listen to you and she talks straight – not always what you want to hear, but it usually makes sense. (girl, 15)

Safe?

'Safe' is a word that many children and young people use about others whom they consider to be trustworthy, to mean that someone can be relied upon as a friend. Its use implies a sense of psychological security.

An important question for everyone reading this book is whether the adult world wants to assist children in feeling 'safe' (as *children* define it) or to ensure that children appear to be 'protected' (as *adults* define it). The former demands flexible, sensitive interventions along the lines of those described by the children whose voices we have recorded. These interventions require adults to respect and keep the confidence and confidentiality of children and young people to a far greater extent than they may be used to doing; it requires adults to countenance much more self-determination by children and young people, which may be experienced as taking even greater risks; and it may require greater trust and faith than either party currently would seem to have for the other.

Conclusions and pointers for practice

Before we began our research, we suspected that many of the children and young people we worked with in our professional lives were moving further away from the adults around them. Sadly, but perhaps more wisely, we are now even more concerned to find so many young people with little or no faith in the adults around them. They doubt our commitment; they doubt our understanding; and they doubt our capacity to be of any use to them when they need us most. And they may have a point. In terms of day-to-day practice, with the aid of Neil Hopkins from the NSPCC, we have devised a statement of principles which we believe goes some way to engaging children in the process of child protection on the basis of what they had told us. We hope you will reflect on this statement and on your own work of protecting children.

Statement of principles

Involvement in what?

- When working with children who have experienced abuse, it is vitally necessary to establish what children themselves see as the primary causes of pain, distress and fear.
- Children's perceptions and fears, as well as acknowledged traumatic events, can have a significant impact on children's lives and well-being, and these need to be addressed and

validated at all stages of investigation, assessment and therapeutic work.
- Child care practitioners should actively address the consequences and associated difficulties resulting from traumatic events experienced by children and pay special attention to the effects of those actions taken specifically to protect the child.

Involvement with whom?

- Children should always be consulted, as part of the negotiation and review of work, to identify any preference they may have regarding the gender, race and culture of their worker.
- Children should always be consulted, as a formal part of any individual programme of work, on their choice of 'Safe' or 'Trusted Person' to support them.
- In allocating and planning work, priority should be given to ensuring continuity of key practitioners/Trusted Persons.

Involvement on whose terms?

- When receiving information from children about their concerns, practitioners/workers should make quite sure that they understand why children are sharing the information and what form of help they require.
- Working agreements with young people should ensure that they retain maximum possible choice/autonomy within the working relationship, while having easy access to advice and support outside it.
- Upon receipt of information from a child about her/himself, practitioners/workers should always consult the young person about their mandate to take action and about the form and content of any such action.
- Clear and understandable 'Confidentiality Contracts' should form part of all work agreements and reviews.

Involvement to what extent?

- In planning work, children should understand and be involved in setting objectives-timescales, which should be realistic, achievable and have meaning/relevance for the young person.
- Work plans/agreements should include a section dedicated to individual children's definition of their problems and the effects that these are having on them.
- Practitioners/Trusted Persons should have the ability to listen to and understand what individual children require, and have the skills to design specific programmes of work to meet their different needs.
- Practitioners/Trusted Persons should ensure that all young people with whom they are working should have the opportunity to contact them in person when they wish/need to do so.
- Practitioners/Trusted Persons should ensure that children are aware of/understand the options available to them during the professional's or other adult's involvement with them.
- Practitioners/Trusted Persons will provide children with information about services that are relevant to their needs, readily understandable and factually correct.

- Children's perception about the reliability and effectiveness of services/service providers should be recorded and addressed in service evaluation and practice supervision.

References

Butler, I. and Williamson, H. (1994) *Children Speak: Children, Trauma and Social Work*. London: Longman, p. 82.

Butler, I. and Williamson, H. (1996) 'Safe?' in Butler, I. and Shaw, I. (eds) *A Case of Neglect: Children's Experiences and the Sociology of Childhood*. Aldershot: Avebury.

CHAPTER 3

CHILDREN'S RIGHTS
David Hodgson

Perhaps the most fundamental change in child care over the latter part of the 20th century has been the gradual philosophical shift from regarding children as objects of concern towards recognising their rights as human beings. Children's rights, including the right to be involved in decisions affecting them, are now enshrined in international law and have been established in all but name within domestic child care legislation. One of the cornerstones of the United Nations Convention on the Rights of the Child 1989, ratified by the UK Government along with most other countries in the world, requires parties to

> assure to the child who is capable of forming his or her own views the right to express those views freely in all matters affecting the child, the views of the child being given due weight in accordance with the age and maturity of the child.
> (Article 12)

The Convention goes on to specify that, in this regard, children 'shall be provided the opportunity to be heard in *any* judicial and administrative proceedings'. [my italics] Nevertheless scepticism remains, even among some child care professionals, as to the wisdom of embracing a children's rights agenda. This chapter acknowledges such doubts while presenting a positive case for recognising and utilising the concept of children's rights. It plots changing definitions of children's rights and considers some of the implications for social work with children and their families.

What is the problem with rights?

There are several reasons for reservations about children's rights, including an enduring sense of unease about human rights in general. 'Rights' can be considered 'wrong' for people, perceived either as unearned entitlements or, from a different standpoint, an apology for self-interest at the expense of co-operation.

Beyond these general concerns, two recurring sources of doubt about children's rights remain: first, a reluctance to accept that children as a group have a valid claim to the possession of rights and, more pragmatically, qualms about whether the notion of children's rights is of any practical relevance for children and their families.

Such doubts reflect a very particular conception of children's rights. Essentially the problem lies in the paradox that rights, especially children's rights, tend to be articulated by those who have the power to define and who, in practice, have the least want of rights. Arguably, the contribution of children and young people to the development of a children's rights movement in the UK has been consistently underplayed. For example, relatively little acknowledgement is given to organisations such as National Association of Young People in Care (NAYPIC) and Black and In Care, which campaigned with some success for protection and participation rights under the Children Act 1989. Hopefully, children's rights are most enduring where children and young people participate in defining them.

What is the use of children's rights?

Rights, almost by definition, seem to be rather abstract and difficult to get a handle on. They feel strong on ideals but weak on practicalities. Moreover, rights can appear contradictory, provoking confusion and conflict. For example, how can children have rights to protection as well as rights to self-determination? Furthermore, confusion about the legal status of children's rights makes it more difficult to take the idea seriously. In summary, while the concept of 'children's rights' may have come a long way since the early 1970s when Hillary Clinton (Rodham 1973) described it as 'a slogan in search of a definition', there remains an enduring sense that the concept generates much heat but little light.

So why should children's rights still have currency? Rights can be said to derive from two fundamental principles: first, the principle of equality – rights outlaw prejudice and discrimination, declaring everyone equal before the law; secondly, rights derive from the principle of autonomy – regard for the integrity of every person as a potential choice-maker. Rights entitle persons to respect and dignity, for which no amount of benevolence or compassion is an adequate substitute (Freeman 1992).

Ironically, human rights only become truly significant in situations in which they are denied. They represent a challenge to the oppressive use of power, which alienates people from their personal experience. The concept of children's human rights is concerned with creating conditions for children and young people to define their experiences for themselves. More meaningful as a process of change than a set of abstract principles, it constitutes a movement in which children and young people, individually and collectively, are the principal players. Hence, the right to participation is at the heart of the children's rights project.

Do children experience discrimination?

Being a child, it might be argued, is unlike any other personal characteristic for which protection from discrimination is claimed, such as race, gender and disability. Not only is it a temporary state of affairs but one that everybody has to go through. However, neither of these objections bears close scrutiny. Injustice need not be permanent or inescapable to be harmful. Nor can age-based discrimination be dismissed simply on the basis that everyone is touched by it.

Beyond these general reservations lies a commonly held belief that children are treated differently because the nature of childhood demands it. At its most extreme, this viewpoint suggests that all distinctions between the rights of adults and children are justifiable by reference to physical and psychological characteristics. The main remedy for children, according to O'Neil (1992), is 'to grow up'.

However, this contention is not supported by the available evidence. It does not, for example, account for the disproportionate impact of poverty upon children (Children's Rights Development Unit 1994), nor does it explain why children are the only group of people who legally can be subjected to physical punishment (for example, smacking) from which everyone else is protected by the criminal law on assault.

Discrimination is generally reinforced by pervasive and contradictory stereotypes reflecting deeply ambivalent social attitudes. Children are no exception. They are portrayed at opposite extremes of vulnerability and power – angels in need of protection and demons threatening disorder (Archard 1993).

Conceding the evidence for discrimination against children, sceptics may protest that other forms of bigotry are far more significant. The competitive approach to human rights will be familiar to those concerned with anti-oppressive practice in social work. It overlooks multiple forms of discrimination and offers only a recipe for division and conflict among groups with potentially shared interests. Childhood is a sitting target for the abuse of power, though barely recognised as an 'ism'. Stereotypes surrounding class, disability, gender and race, for example, reflect similar preoccupations with protection and control. But parallels between the struggles of different groups do not make their interests identical. Understanding the distinction can avert misjudgements, for example, in tackling problems of 'domestic violence' (Ennew 1986; Ahmed 1988).

In spite of their unique contribution to the movement for children's rights, young people in care continue to face particular forms of discrimination. 'Careism' (Lindsay 1994) is predicated on a series of stereotypical attitudes about the characteristics and behaviour of young people in care. It permitted abuse in the name of therapy, for example, during the 'Pindown Experience' in Staffordshire and the regime of Frank Beck in Leicestershire. Today it rationalises, for instance, a discriminatory law on secure accommodation, subdued adult expectations of the educational attainment of children 'in care' as well as higher rates of school exclusion, and levels of support for care leavers that are lower than those available to their counterparts in the general population.

Changing definitions of children's human rights

Changing definitions of children's rights are probably best understood with reference to broader movements for the recognition of human rights. International human-rights law remains dominated by Western libertarian conceptions of rights defined as individual freedom from external interference. An alternative view of rights as conditions that enable us to fulfil our human potential places much greater emphasis upon collective experience as a complement to individuality. Traditionally, these two classifications of rights have been strictly separated, with priority given to libertarian freedoms, including civil and political rights, rather than 'group rights' such as the freedoms achieved by improvements in people's material, economic and social lives (Leary 1993).

This conceptual division has been particularly unfortunate in the case of children since it has tended to impede the recognition of certain rights for them. It helps explain why adult supporters of children's rights became grouped into two opposing camps: in crude terms 'protectionists', perceiving childhood as the basis for asserting special interests for a particularly vulnerable group of human beings, are lined up against 'liberationists', who see it as a social construct to deny freedom, using the arbitrary criterion of age (Fox Harding 1991).

Furthermore, in the allocation of human rights, children have been short-changed. On the one hand, libertarian rights generally are viewed as being at odds with stereotypical images of the child, whether as 'angel' or as 'devil'. On the other hand, at first glance it would appear that children's collective rights to have their 'best interests' protected are acknowledged more readily. Certainly this is a key principle both of the Children Act 1989 and the UN Convention 1989. The problem here, however, is that it is relatively easy to declare a commitment to the child's best interests without specifying precisely what it is. As Eekelaar (1994) has documented, the notion of 'best interests' historically has been used to enable power holders (generally men), to keep the least powerful, including women and children, in subjugation.

However, the current (some would say, restrictive) definition of children's rights to welfare and protection has at least two important side effects. First, it is arguable that it contributes to doubts among families and communities as to authenticity of agency aspirations to 'partnership'. For example, Jones (1994) draws attention to disillusionment among black communities arising from neglect of the abusive impact of racism on children, asserting that 'by its failure to address racial violence, social work is sanctioning it'. Moreover, evidence of the disproportionate use of compulsory social work intervention among families living below the official poverty line (Bebbington and Miles 1989) is suggestive of a child protection system applying exclusively individualised remedies to problems that are at least partially structural in origin.

There is a second problem associated with the limited notion of children's welfare or protection rights, namely that it tends to bolster the belief that children can only gain rights at their parents' expense. By a relatively small leap of the imagination, children's rights can be depicted as a threat to 'family values'.

Under the Children Act 1989 parental rights were converted into responsibilities by the addition of 'duties' to children. This was a significant symbolic departure from the doctrine of children as parental possessions. Yet the nature of the responsibility was not spelled out, allowing the reciprocal responsibilities of the state towards parents to remain relatively ill-defined. Part III of the Act prefers social work discretion rather than complementary rights of support for children and parents.

The issue of children's rights raises fundamental concerns about the balance of power within families, including the question of how 'family' is defined. The Children Act 1989 reflects a broader notion of 'family' than previously recognised, thus opening up new possibilities for challenging the parental monopoly over decision-making. However, in spite of provisions in the Act ostensibly designed to bring public and private family law into closer alignment, there is still a robust resistance, fortified by case law, towards challenges to parental authority in the absence of firm evidence pointing to significant harm. In fact, courts are not even required to apply the welfare principle to parental decision-making when separating or divorcing couples agree on child care arrangements, notwithstanding objections from the children.

Participation and choice for young people

The United Nations Convention on the Rights of the Child 1989, though conceived by relatively powerful adults, represents a challenge to orthodox thinking about human rights. It is almost as if the predicament of children highlighted some of the contradictions within traditional approaches to human rights. The Convention transcends the artificial divide between individual and collective, negative and positive rights. Social, economic and cultural rights are placed alongside civil and political rights as mutually indispensable, notwithstanding the priority accorded to negative rights at the insistence of Western signatories to the Convention (Article 4). Children's human rights only make practical sense when this mutuality is recognised. For example, the right to freedom of association is of limited value without adequate transport systems and a safe, accessible environment. This exposes the mythology surrounding self-determination, whether for children or to adults.

Under the Convention, and less expansively within the Children Act 1989, the right to participation provides a key to ensuring that judgements about welfare demonstrate respect for the child as an individual with her or his own preferences. Such is the difficulty in coming to terms with the validity of children's views and feelings that, in spite of legal requirements for consultation, they are still frequently overlooked or, alternatively, dismissed as being at odds with our own view of what is best for the child.

It could be argued that both the UN Convention and the Children Act have manoeuvred carefully around what, for many, remains the critical question posed by Eekelaar – 'How can acting towards children with the objective of furthering their best interests be reconciled with treating children as possessors of rights?' – if following this imperative entails having complete power over the child? Here, two questions tend to become muddled: first, whether and under what circumstances children should have a right to make decisions independent of their parents or carers; and, secondly, whether, in spite of parental objection or permission, the courts representing the state as *parens patriae* (or supreme parent) should be able to override the child's wishes. The principle of child autonomy established in the *Gillick* case (*Gillick v West Norfolk and Wisbech Health Authority* 1985 3 All ER402) has been undermined by subsequent legal judgements on both issues.

In addition, there are different ways of approaching judgements of this kind. For example, one can distinguish between, on the one hand, the 'mature minor' doctrine, espoused by Lord Scarman in *Gillick* and, on the other, a 'fixed age' approach to child emancipation. The former requires careful assessment of the child's level of understanding regardless of age, whereas the latter amounts to a presumption of competence that can only be refuted with contrary evidence. Currently English law attempts to straddle these two approaches.

Theoretical and practical solutions have been put forward in response to the apparent conflict between the right to protection and the right to autonomy. For example, Freeman (1992) proposes the idea of 'future-oriented consent', a form of substituted judgement requiring those making crucial decisions on behalf of a child to project themselves into the future in order to estimate what the child would have judged her or his interests to be. Eekelaar (1994) instead suggests 'dynamic self-determinism', the 'creation of space' for children to play a progressively more active role in otherwise adult-oriented decision-making structures, principally through greater emphasis on open-ended decisions. (Both approaches seem increasingly to feature in professional and judicial decision-making.) Arguably, however, these models continue to rely on stereotypes of children as essentially isolated, self-absorbed creatures rather than human beings who interact in complex and reciprocal relationships with their families and friends.

The notion of competence would also appear to have been influenced by questionable assumptions about children. At least three issues are relevant here. First, children's competence tends to be systematically underestimated. For instance, a review of research in child psychology led one prominent commentator (Donaldson 1978) to conclude, 'at least from the age of four . . . . we must acknowledge that the supposed gap between children and adults is less than many have claimed'. Secondly, the impact of expectations often is neglected. Adults in particular have a direct impact on children's competencies in two ways: through control over opportunities to demonstrate competence and by the emotional pull of expectations (Solberg 1990). Thirdly, the assumption that there is an objective way of measuring competence is not borne out in practice. The assumption of objectivity in assessments of children's competence can detract from more personal and subjective aspects of choice-making, such as the beliefs, hopes and fears linked to particular options. Believing that you have made the right choice is likely to have a genuine impact on the outcome.

Commentators differ as to the value of 'competence' as a way of regulating children's claims to autonomy, particularly in the context of decisions involving risk to health and well-being. For example, Lansdown (1995) argues in favour of children's rights to make autonomous choices based on assessed competence, asserting that this should be overridden only where the child is exposed to serious risk. Schofield and Thoburn (1996), on the other hand, cite a number of objections to the notion of competence in 'child protection' cases. They include difficulties in assessing child competence within the dynamics of abusive relationships, the danger of labelling children as competent or incompetent and the burden of responsibility placed upon the shoulders of the child. These are important pragmatic considerations. They do not negate the notion of child competence, nor the principle of allowing children choice, even where the risks of harm may be considerable. However, a serious practical difficulty with the notion of competence is that often those who have responsibility for assessing competence (whether the social worker, guardian *ad litem* or other specialist) also have to decide what is best for the child. In these circumstances it may be beyond professional competence to distinguish unequivocally between these two issues when the burden of responsibility is so great. Separating the two assessments in some way might offer a way forward.

Consultation with young people about children's rights suggests that self-determination may be more of a 'hang-up' for adults than for children. I recently interviewed groups of young people aged 9 and upwards (1998); they put a great deal of store by mutual respect in relationships with adults and peers alike. Being acknowledged as a giver as well as a receiver, being taken seriously, and being treated with honesty and fairness were also high on young people's agendas. In this context, recognition of child competence is an important point in principle as well as in practice. As Alderson and Goodwin (1993) conclude: 'Treating children as if they are competent can encourage their latent abilities, including the sense to know when to leave decisions to other people.'

References

Ahmed, S. (1988) 'Defining and assessing black families' in *Planning for Children*. London: Family Rights Group, pp. 9–18.

Alderson, P. and Goodwin, M. (1993) 'Contradictions within concepts of competence', *International Journal of Children's Rights,* 1.3, p. 306.

Archard, D. (1993) *Rights and Childhood.* London: Routledge.

Arnstein, S. (1969) 'A ladder of citizen participation', *Journal of the American Institute of Planners,* 35, pp. 216–24.

Bebbington, A and Miles, J. (1989) 'The background of children who enter local authority care', *The British Journal of Social Work*, 19, no. 5.

Children's Rights Development Unit (1994) *The UK Agenda for Children.* London: Gulbenkian Foundation.

Department of Health (1993) *Guidance on Permissible Forms of Control in Children's Residential Care.* London: HMSO.

Donaldson, M. (1978) *Children's Minds.* London: Fontana/Croom Helm.

Eekelaar, J. (1994) 'The Interests of the Child and the Role of Dynamic Self-Determinism', *International Journal of Law and the Family,* 8, pp. 42–61.

Ennew, J. (1986) *The Sexual Exploitation of Children.* Cambridge: Polity Press.

Fox Harding, L.M. (1991) 'The Children Act in Context: Four perspectives in child care law and policy', *Journal of Social Welfare and Family Law,* 1, 3, pp. 179–93.

Freeman, M. (1992) 'The Limits of Children's Rights' in Freeman, M. and Veerman, P. (eds) *The Ideologies of Children's Rights.* Amsterdam: Martinus Nijhoff.

Hodgson, D. (1998) *Promoting Children's Rights in Practice – Pointers for Child Care Agencies Committed to Children's Rights.* London: National Council for Voluntary Child Care Organisations.

Jones, A. (1994) 'Anti-racist child protection' in David, T., *Protecting Children from Abuse.* London: Trentham Books.

Lansdown, G. (1995) *Taking Part: children's participation in decision making.* London: Institute for Public Policy Research.

Leary, V. (1993) 'The Social and Economic Rights of the Child' in *Selected Essays on Children's Rights.* London: Defence for Children International, p. 25.

Lindsay, M. (1994) 'An introduction to children's rights' in *Seen and Heard.* London: National Association of Guardians *ad Litem* and Reporting Officers.

O'Neil, O. (1992) 'Children's Rights and Children's Lives', *International Journal of Law and the Family,* 6, p. 39.

Rodham, H. (1973) 'Children Under the Law', *Harvard Education Review,* 43, p. 487.

Schofield, G. and Thoburn, J. (1996) *'The Voice of the Child: Participation in Decision Making'*. London: Institute for Public Policy Research.

Solberg, A. (1990) 'Negotiating Childhood' in James, A. and Prout, A. (eds) *Constructing and Reconstructing Childhood.* Brighton: Falmer Press.

CHAPTER 4

PLANNING AND REVIEWING WITH CHILDREN IN SUBSTITUTE CARE
Yvonne Shemmings

If proof were needed that involving children and young people in planning is not straightforward, it was inadvertently illustrated to me recently by a small group of young people planning to celebrate the birthday of one of their friends. Everyone was excited and enthusiastic. Lots of ideas were suggested about where to go (although anxiety about not being admitted to certain places at times dominated). The group agonised over transport arrangements, the cost of the evening and the new clothes that had to be bought if they were to be allowed in the places they had chosen. And it seemed they all wanted something different from the evening. Some were excited at the prospect of romance; others at a wild night dancing; still others saw it as an opportunity to buy some new clothes. But it quickly became obvious that one person had stayed silent throughout the excited chatter, and gradually, as the obstacles looked insurmountable it seemed that, for her, much of the sheen had been taken off the event. A hush descended over them; suddenly, a quiet voice spoke: 'I only really wanted a gathering at my house with my friends anyway.' They all laughed at the simplicity of this; and it seemed that a burden had been lifted.

The person who made this stunning suggestion was, of course, the 'birthday girl' herself. Up until then no one had thought to ask her what *she* wanted, and in the excitement they had completely forgotten that she was the key person to consider when making the plans. She had ceased to be 'at the centre'. However, after her revelation the preferred 'outcome' was established: to arrange an evening to celebrate; chosen by the 'birthday girl'; with people invited whom *she* wanted; and at minimum expense. And finally, of course, that a wonderful time would be had by all. Once this preference had been established, the task became easier and, having placed the most important person first, attention continued to focus on her in a genuine attempt to find out about what *she* wanted for her birthday celebration.

Listening to this discussion, I found striking similarities with systems for planning and reviewing with children 'looked after' by the local authority. Anyone involved in plans and reviews undoubtedly begins with good intentions, and few professionals would question the importance of good planning for children and young people. However, not all professionals are confident about involving them in the process, even though most will say that they believe in the principle.

This chapter describes briefly the legislative background – it is covered more fully by Steve Walker in Chapter 6 – behind involving children and young people in their plans and reviews, discusses why it is considered important, and concludes by outlining some practical ways of increasing their participation.

Legislative background

The Children Act 1989, together with accompanying Guidance documents, emphasises the importance of working in partnership with parents, carers and other agencies, but whilst the Review of Children's Cases Regulations gives children and young people who are looked after or accommodated by a local authority the right to have their voices heard in relation to plans made about their future, it does not go beyond advising 'consultation' about their wishes and feelings. Again, even though the Guidance indicates that good practice would dictate that attendance at reviews should be the norm, nevertheless there is no legal right for the young person to do so. It is at the discretion of the local authority whether s/he is considered to be of 'an appropriate age and understanding' to attend. Pressurised workers juggling their priorities within caseloads may be tempted only to adhere to the bare minimum regarding the 'consultation' guidance, or simply not do it at all.

Why plan?

Children growing up in their family may never be aware of 'plans' being made with them or about them. Their experience of 'plans' is likely to be objectively different from children growing up in public care, who often face numerous changes about where they live and who looks after them. They have to talk to social workers about themselves and their experiences and have much of this information made available to other people, for example their teachers at school. In short, they are exposed to many things (far beyond what brought them into care) that are not normally experienced by other children. As a result it is possible that they are assumed to be well-versed in the 'system' and to have a sophisticated understanding of public care and, consequently, that they are well aware of what will happen to them. But much of the anecdotal evidence and research concludes that many young people in the care system feel completely uninvolved in decisions affecting their lives; that they are unable to influence their future; and that people come and go with only a sporadic and fleeting interest in them. Many youngsters simply give up trying to be involved and this is then reflected in their behaviour, thus compounding the views of professionals that they are not of an 'age and understanding' to participate in decision-making processes.

It is these differences that have been exposed in various studies into the experiences of children looked after by the local authority and have resulted in the publication of recent Department of Health (1995) materials for use with such children, in order to improve outcomes with them. The system is designed to enhance the involvement of young people by encouraging carers to work *with* them, not just for them. The aim is to gather important information about young people, find out what is important to them, gauge their wishes and feelings, and then make plans together for the future based upon such information.

Involving children and young people in the planning process is important for other reasons too. Recent court cases have demonstrated that those persons responsible for parenting in the public care system increasingly are made more accountable for their mistakes. Children experiencing the public care system are beginning to challenge decisions made on their behalf during their time in care. In adulthood some are claiming damages by saying, in effect, 'I blame you for the way I am,' or, 'You are responsible for not giving me the opportunities I deserved.' Rarely do children take their own parents to court for their failings, but increasingly adults who were brought up in public care are challenging omissions and wrong decisions made during

Planning and Reviewing with Children in Substitute Care

their childhood and adolescence. The move towards accountability in the field of public parenting serves to remind practitioners and managers of the awesome responsibility placed on them to parent children well. One young person poignantly wondered, 'If all you people, with all your education and knowledge, can't bring us up properly, what hope is there?'

Practical ways of involving children

Imagine or reflect back to this scenario for a moment. You are 9 years old and you are sitting in your class in your primary school. You live with foster parents. You have been invited to a child care review meeting. You were told on what day and at what time it will take place. You will have to leave school early because one or two of the adults who are coming do not work after 3.30 and your foster carer has to collect other children from school at 3.15. The last time you went to such a meeting they blamed you for not doing the things you promised you would (even though you believed nothing would change for you after the meeting). Your teacher will be there again and will hear about what one of your parents did to you and how you are coping with 'the therapy sessions'. What is more, the school nurse and the social worker always argue with each other. You do not know who else will be there. From what you can remember about the last meeting, half the time they seemed to be catching up on each other's news and had their noses buried in reports (which you had not seen). You remember that the chairs were uncomfortable; at the moment, you are hungry and thirsty.

This description is not a particularly unusual scenario for children who are looked after by local authorities and, although it seems like part of a nightmare, it is a description one young person described recently to me.

Involving children requires time, patience and skill. With some children you may need to use pictures, books, toys and dolls, or make comparisons with other situations that they find helpful. Plan what you are going to say and go well-prepared; give it as much attention as you would with other direct work with a child.

Do not give false expectations about what will happen as a result of a planning or review meeting. Do not say it will be 'fun', when it is not likely to be. Be realistic and reassuring. Tell the child who needs to be part of the process and why. For example, if a teacher 'needs to know', perhaps you could say something like 'The last time we all met there were some things worrying you, which your teacher felt could be stopping you from concentrating at school, and it is important to hear from her to see if this has changed.' Children should be able to choose whether they want to be in the room to hear this, or whether they would like to go into the meeting after the teacher had spoken or after s/he has left. They could be asked if they want a teacher to stay for the whole meeting. If this is the case the meeting can be broken down into small 'chunks', perhaps with other people attending in stages but still ensuring that those who need to meet together can still do so.

Find out from the young person what time of day s/he feels at their best; do not assume that taking a child out of school is *always* the wrong thing to do. Discuss it with the child. If the child finds difficulty expressing a view, you could work out a range of options together and then ask the child to give you 'points out of ten' for each one according to how near s/he thinks you are to the chosen preference.

When plans and decisions are being considered about the future, tell the child that s/he is the most important person. If this involves a meeting, then help children to understand that is not just about them, it is *for* them. But this can feel like a big responsibility for some young people, who may decide that they do not want to come. If this is the case, and s/he does not wish to go to any part of the meeting or be seen at all by others in the room, then s/he may prefer just to sit outside the door. S/he could be asked if s/he wants anyone whom s/he likes or trusts to go out from time to time, to let her or him know what has been said and to ask if s/he wants to relay anything back into the meeting.

The reports of those attending should be discussed with children well before the meeting, not on the same day. This gives them a chance to question what has been said and to write (or draw) their own report for the meeting. This should be given to the person chairing the review, also in advance and along with the other reports.

The choice of venue is important too. Not only is it seen as stigmatising by some people to arrive in a social services office to wait in a reception area for the meeting to begin, it is not conducive to a young person waiting there. Receptionists should be advised about who is expected to attend, so that people waiting do not have to go into lengthy explanations in front of others. Ideally, the venue should be in a neutral place where refreshments are available and which is comfortable.

Young people need to know how long the meeting will last and whether there will be a break after a specified time. It is useful to rehearse anything that is likely to lead to difficult feelings for the child (such as anger or pain) by predicting them in advance, and then perhaps role-playing such situations in a safe environment. They should be told in advance that, if they get upset in the meeting and feel that they want to leave, then there can be a short break to enable them to talk privately about their feelings. They can then return later, if they feel up to it, or they may prefer to pass on what they want to say to someone whom they trust to tell the others in the meeting.

Children from other cultures must have access to interpreter services if necessary, as well as being able to invite a friend or advocate; children with disabilities often will require specialist help to ensure that their wishes and feelings are represented properly and appropriately. A more detailed account of the issues involved in empowering such children can be found in a variety of training packs, an example being the *ABCD Pack* by Kennedy and Gordon (1993).

A letter should be sent to young people thanking them if they felt able to go, or acknowledging that they did not attend but telling them they can come to subsequent meetings if they change their mind in future. A brief outline of the meeting in straightforward language should be included in this letter. Some children will feel upset when they get it, and so carers should be made aware of what the child will be receiving in order that they can support the young person, by reading it through if necessary or by being there to answer any questions.

The minutes of the meeting should be in a form that the child understands, but should not be patronising. The decisions should be clear and separated from the body of the minutes. Some young people prefer to have the same minutes as everyone else sent to them. A tape-recording or video could be made, or a booklet written especially for them. A simple notebook is sometimes useful, especially if it is added to at subsequent meetings. It may be that a personal calendar can be drawn, for them to see what will happen and when.

Conclusion

Involving children in plans and reviews is not an event; it is both a process and an ideological concept. In reality, many children and young people who are 'looked after' are not always visited regularly by a social worker, and therefore involvement cannot be based solely on the 'relationship' with the worker. In this sense it is not completely necessary for there to be a strong and long-standing relationship for successful involvement to occur. However, by involving children and young people, trust is more likely to develop.

Each negative experience of 'social services' for a young person adds to her or his pool of similar experiences and thus affects her or his reaction to being involved in planning and review processes. Workers should be sensitive to this but try to ensure that any passivity, apathy or disinterest is not seen as being permanent. One good experience of a planning or review process can open other doors, so that young people then want to become more active in other decisions about their life. However, it is not enough simply to hear their views; those views must be given credence, thought and consideration. If their wishes cannot be fulfilled, then reasons and explanations should be given. When their views conflict with those of the professionals, their wishes should not be minimised but should form the basis of discussion and future work with each young person. Any objections should be noted in the minutes of the meeting.

Young people often say that they want to discover and understand what options are available to them as well as what the consequences of each option might be. They then want to think about this on their own and make their choice. Some say that they want to know which option the worker would choose *if that worker were in the child's shoes*. What they do not like is to be told what they are going to do, or what is going to happen to them, without knowing why or what the alternatives are.

Finally, involving children and young people in the planning and reviewing processes can help build trusting relationships and lead the way to better outcomes for children looked after in the public care system, and perhaps offer workers some of the elusive job satisfaction that may have become even more obscured in these times of increasing public criticism.

References

Department of Health (1995) *Looking After Children*. London: HMSO.

Kennedy, M. and Gordon, R. (1993) *The ABCD Pack – ABuse and Children Who are Disabled*. London: Way Ahead Disability Consultancy/NSPCC/National Deaf Children's Society/Chailey Heritage.

CHAPTER 5

RESEARCH INTO CHILDREN'S INVOLVEMENT IN CHILD PROTECTION CONFERENCES
David Shemmings

In this chapter I present an overview of the findings from two research studies into the involvement of children and young people in child protection conferences undertaken between 1993 and 1994 in two local authorities, one in an inner-London borough ('Wyeboro') and the other in a large county in the south of England ('Exshire'). Although I refer in general terms to the views of children and young people, the main focus of this chapter is on the professionals, the people chairing the conferences and the parents or carers. Only an overview of the findings is possible here, but a more detailed account of the research is available elsewhere (Shemmings 1996) and in this book it is discussed in Chapter 14 by Nicky Scutt and in Chapter 15 by Dee Lynes and her colleagues.

Background to the research

Both Exshire and Wyeboro were interested in studying the results of a policy of regularly and routinely inviting young people to child protection conferences. The policy in Wyeboro was to invite children to both initial and review conferences, whereas in Exshire the decision was taken to invite them only to reviews. In Exshire, only one area of the county was included in the study; in Wyeboro, the whole of the borough took part. Both authorities wanted to gauge the views of the children, their parents or carers, the professionals and those chairing the meetings. In terms of research methodology this gave us an opportunity to use the principles of 'triangulation', that is, looking at the same phenomenon from three or more different perspectives: there is one conference, but each group of social actors places significance on different aspects of it. Each phase of the research was designed in conjunction with the two authorities, especially concerning anti-oppressive practice.

The key research question to the adults in this study was 'What are your views about *this child* who has attended?' rather than 'What do you think about *children in general* attending conferences?' Thus, although the research is indirectly a study of attitudes, first and foremost it seeks to shed light on the phenomenon of children's involvement by looking at the reaction of adults to its *actual* occurrence.

It was agreed that I would study the first 20 or so conferences to which a young person had been invited (whether or not s/he then decided to attend). The young people were asked if they would agree to be interviewed, irrespective of whether they went to the meeting. To find out the reactions of the adults, they were asked to complete a questionnaire. The aim of the research, however, was not to count variables, add up data and conduct statistical tests, but to *understand phenomena*. Thus, a qualitative approach was used in this study rather than a quantitative one. Because in nearly all respects there are no significant differences between the two authorities, for the most part the data have been combined.

Contextual data

Although the data were studied qualitatively, nevertheless it is important to appreciate the overall context. A total of 47 young people were invited to the conferences, of whom 38 attended and then 34 agreed to be interviewed by a researcher. The number of questionnaires completed by the professionals was 121, giving a response rate of over 80 per cent. A slightly lower rate in respect of the parents or carers (around 70 per cent) left us with 23 completed questionnaires.

I was fortunate to achieve a high response rate from those chairing the conferences. The 34 completed questionnaires contain rich and fascinating information, which will be of interest to people chairing all types of meetings in the context of family support and child protection; equally, they are relevant to other professionals, and to children and young people.

From the 34 conferences for which we have corresponding information from the chairperson: in 27 the young person was present throughout; 20 lasted for more than an hour; in 26 conferences a parent or carer attended too, and at no time was asked to leave; and the actual or alleged abuser was present in 12 of the meetings. But in only three of the conferences did the young person have an independent advocate to provide support.

In terms of the ages of the 38 children and young people who attended, four were aged 12 or less, seven were 13, seven were 14, and twenty were aged 15 or over. Of the young people attending, 16 were male and 22 were female.

Regarding the ethnicity of the children (and using the categories agreed with the inner-London authority), 29 were white British, 3 were black British, 2 were white Irish, 1 was white Irish/Argentinian and 3 were of dual heritage. A large portion of each questionnaire explored the extent to which the 'race', culture, religion, language, disability, age and gender of the young person were, when relevant, taken into account. Respondents usually answered these questions in a thoughtful way, as the following example illustrates:

> The child is white British and his first language is English. The majority of the conference members were white British too and it was conducted in English. There were no issues presenting relative to sexuality or gender. He presented as appropriately articulate and mature for his age. All the conference members appeared supportive and sensitive to his needs. (Shemmings 1996)

Because the policy in Wyeboro was different from that in Exshire in terms of the types of conferences held and the decisions made, I shall now separate the data for the two authorities. In Exshire, where all conferences attended by children were *review* not *initial* meetings, out of the total of 16 children who attended it was decided to register 9 children and to remove the names of 7. In Wyeboro there were six initial conferences involving children, at which one child was placed on the register, three children were not and for two children a decision was deferred pending further information; in addition there were 12 review conferences at which 5 names were removed and 7 were registered.

Finally, there was a wide range of abuse registered at the conferences: 9 children were registered for 'sexual abuse', 12 for 'emotional abuse', 3 for 'physical abuse', and 4 as 'neglect', with the remaining children either being registered as a combined category (or not registered at all).

The main reason for putting these findings in context is that one of the concerns of some practitioners and managers is that only those conferences likely to conform to the 'best scenario' will be selected for children to attend (see Thoburn *et al* 1995 for a description of the concept of 'best' and 'worst' scenario applied to family participation in child protection). The fear is that, as a result of professionals' concerns about the presence of children in conferences, they might seek to exclude them from any meeting which 'on paper' looked more difficult. For example, they might exclude children from conferences if the alleged or actual abuser is going to be present; if sexual abuse is alleged; or if the parent or carer does not admit the allegations; and so on. The background data outlined above illustrate that neither of the two authorities selected 'best scenario' cases when deciding which children to invite.

Views of the professionals

Rather than present the reader with each of the relevant percentages, I aim to capture the essence of the findings in the following summary. Nevertheless, the overwhelming impression that which one is left with after studying the 121 questionnaires is just how consistently positive are the results. Two overall findings confirm this impression. First, at the end of the questionnaire respondents were asked to indicate whether, on the whole and in respect of the specific children and young people who had attended, their impressions were positive or negative. Of the 121 responses, 111 were positive, 6 were negative and 4 were classified as 'guarded' or 'neutral'. Secondly, to the question *'Did you think that the child was of a sufficient age and understanding to attend the meeting?'* 117 answered 'Yes' and only 4 said 'No'.

Professionals in this study probably were no more 'for' or 'against' involving children than any similar group elsewhere in the country. Most groups of adults will contain marked variations in attitudes to this example of giving children a voice in decision-making. What the findings suggest is that the *actual practice* of involving young people is far less problematic than is feared, a finding that many readers will remember is exactly what happened when parents started to attend conferences. This is not to say, however, that there were no difficulties; indeed, the full analysis of the findings deliberately concentrates upon those difficulties as well as other important dilemmas and the challenges for professional practice in the future (Shemmings 1996).

At a more specific level of analysis the overwhelming majority: knew before the meeting that a child had been invited, or if they did not they nevertheless agreed with the reason given at the start of the meeting; thought they had not withheld information merely because a child was in the room, or that if there was something that they needed to say without the young person present then they worked out a way of doing so; and, when asked to think back to the meeting afterwards, did not think there was anything that they would have said differently.

If the child spoke at the meeting, then professionals thought it was relevant to its purpose. This last finding can be broken down in more detail. They were asked to rate on a seven-point scale the extent to which they thought that the young person's presence at the meeting helped

(=7) or hindered (=1) the process. Most of the scores were between 5.0 and 5.5, suggesting that the child's involvement was thought to be broadly helpful, but that – and as many of those responding to the questionnaire said – 'their presence in the room made no difference to the purpose of the meeting'. By this, professionals did not mean that the child's involvement was irrelevant; what they meant was that the child's presence in the room did not prevent them 'from doing their job of protecting the young person'.

Although the vast majority (113 out of 121) thought that there were clear benefits for the child being in the conference, when asked whether they thought there were any problems for the children a difference of opinion emerged: 55 said 'Yes' and 66 said 'No'. This difference reflects the ways in which professionals interpreted any discomfort shown by a child when in the room. If, for example, a child looked anxious or worried, then some professionals concluded that this was a 'problem' for the child. Interestingly, most of the young people interviewed said that although the meeting was stressful, and that this could have been reduced significantly if they had been prepared properly, nevertheless they went on to say – to quote one young person: 'I'm glad that I came . . . . but I wouldn't say that I enjoyed it . . . . and I wouldn't want to go to too many too often!'

Finally, I wanted to find out if any professionals had stopped coming to conferences because a child might be there. Consequently, professionals who did not attend the conference (but who had been invited) were asked to give their reasons. Amongst the 59 replies there were no examples of anyone saying that it was the result of a child being invited.

Views of the persons chairing the meetings

Professionals rated very highly the chairperson's skill in handling the conference when the child was present and emphasised the pivotal nature of the role. Chairpersons themselves did not doubt the complexities involved in handling this meeting with the young person there. Child protection conferences are difficult enough to chair with just professionals present; what would it be like now with parents *and* their children in the room?

These anxieties appeared in the results. Of the 34 chairpersons who replied, 18 said they experienced difficulties handling the meeting with the child there. These difficulties included: when an alleged abuser protested his innocence; when dealing with information about an older brother; when the chairperson thought that a girl was putting on an 'act of reassurance' about feeling safe, but only because she was frightened of the abuser; and having to say critical things about a mother's ability to bring up her son, for fear of undermining her in front of him. Equally difficult were those situations when children or parents, or both, became upset or angry.

Overall, most people chairing conferences said that they were not worried about the young person being there (27 said they were not, 7 said that they were). And, like the professionals questioned, they thought that the child was of 'an age and understanding' to have been there.

Views of the parents or carers

The questionnaire was answered by 23 parents or carers and included: 10 mothers (or stepmothers); 7 fathers (or stepfathers); three examples when both parents came; one other relative; and 2 foster carers. Perhaps surprisingly – but this is where the small size of the cohort needs to be taken into account – the views of parents and carers were very positive. For example, 20 said they thought that their child was treated well, 22 said that *they* were treated well and 19 said they thought the professionals in the meeting were 'open and honest'. Many people made a distinction referred to in other studies: being 'open and honest' is not the same as being 'nice'; like most of us, I suspect, parents wanted professionals to show all three qualities. One parent said that she was good at telling the difference between,

> .... a worker who is just trying to be nice, and others who are being straight with me – not that I agreed with them mind .... I just appreciated it when they were fair and honest but kind. (Shemmings 1996)

Conclusion

Children and young people often display considerable insight into their own needs. A short anecdote that someone told me from a different authority will illustrate this. But a word of explanation first. One of the interesting developments in practice resulting from this research was a model to help children work out their precise needs for involvement. The model consists of a working application of the mathematical combinations of four key variables involved in any form of participation: when we decide whether to become 'involved' with others, intuitively we ask ourselves: (a) if we want to 'see' what is happening; (b) whether we want to be 'seen'; (c) whether we want to 'hear' what is going on; and (d) whether we want to be 'heard'. One of the reasons why participation and involvement are such complicated forms of human interaction is because the 4 variables combine in 16 different ways. This model is explained in more detail in the training pack *In On The Act* (Shemmings 1996).

So, to the anecdote. A young child was thinking about how and whether he wanted to be involved in a child protection conference. Eventually he decided that he did – but that he wanted to sit under the table. By asking to do this he implied that he wanted to 'hear others but not see them, and to speak but not be seen by the adults'. When I have put this particular combination of the four *Participation Variables* to groups of professionals during training sessions on children's participation, we have always concluded that (a) it requires a 'live' audio-link into the room and that (b) as a consequence it would be unlikely to be an option at most venues. But here is a child who has found a perfectly feasible way to get his needs met.

Unfortunately, the boy was not allowed to sit under the table because it was thought that he 'only wanted to do it to muck about'. Perhaps he did; but why not give him a chance and see? Otherwise adults will yet again, and with equal justification, be open to the accusation that they do not listen to young people. And what an opportunity this was for the adults to help him see how important it might be not to 'muck about' in the meeting. Talking of children 'mucking about', I wonder if the professional(s) who decided that he could not sit under the table were forgetting their own experiences when young; or, perhaps, even when not so young. I wonder too if they had forgotten that when children are frightened, or when they have little reason to trust adults, they tend to express their desperation and pain in mucky ways.

This example also illustrates one of the key findings from this research, namely that the successful involvement of young people in child protection processes rests upon two key factors: the *preparedness* and *resilience* of the child.

Although the results of the study are positive – indeed, it is true to say that it was only three or four specific conferences that absorbed the majority of the negative comments – it is wise to try to draw out from the research the main problem areas so that children and young people can be given a louder voice in the future, not just in child protection conferences, or even in meetings generally, but throughout all family support and child protection processes.

References

Shemmings, D. (1996) *Involving Children in Child Protection Conferences*, Social Work Monographs, No.152. Norwich: University of East Anglia.

Thoburn, T., Lewis, A. and Shemmings, D. (1995) *Paternalism or Partnership? Family Involvement in the Child Protection Process*. London: HMSO, p. 34.

CHAPTER 6

CHILDREN'S PERSPECTIVES ON ATTENDING STATUTORY REVIEWS
Steve Walker

In 1995 I conducted a small-scale, intensive qualitative study of 15 young people who had been involved, to some extent, in 'plans and reviews' within the 'looked after' children system. I used materials designed to strengthen existing planning systems (Department of Health 1995). To support the introduction of the materials, a group consultation session was held for young people aged between 12 and 15 during the summer holidays. Invitations were sent to all children 'looked after' and a total of 17 attended. The agenda for the afternoon was set by them. Although they were interested and positive about the materials, they also wanted to use part of the session to talk about their experiences of review meetings.

As a result of the views obtained through the initial consultation, it was decided to undertake a further research project to explore their involvement in the planning and review process.

Information on the research project was sent out to all children 'looked after', over the age of 12, as those in this age group were always invited to their review meeting. They were asked to participate in an individual interview with a researcher. Participants self-selected, either by contacting the researcher directly, or through their carer or social worker. A total of 15 young people were seen, including children in long- and short-term foster and residential placements.

To help the children to feel they were in control of the process, the interviews were conducted in a place and at a time that suited them. Most of those interviewed were happy to be seen where they were living but five children requested that the interview took place elsewhere. Only one did not keep the appointment. It was explained to those interviewed that they could bring a relative, carer or friend with them. In the research, one young person was seen with a friend and two sibling groups of two were interviewed together. To allow the children the scope and opportunity to talk, the interviews did not have a pre-set list of questions but were conducted on a semi-structured basis around the main themes identified in the initial consultation. This approach proved to be highly successful and many participants appeared to welcome the opportunity to talk without interruption. The themes identified were developed as the series of interviews progressed.

All those children interviewed were happy for to be tape-recorded. They were reassured that they could stop the interview at any time, or ask the researcher to move on to a different area if they felt uncomfortable in any way with the discussion. In the event it was generally the researcher who was left feeling uncomfortable that the review meetings were such a difficult experience.

The planning and review system

The current system of planning for children 'looked after' was established by the Children Act 1989. The Act requires local authorities to draw up an individual Care Plan, to promote and safeguard the welfare of every child they look after. The plan must be in writing and should be reviewed at regular intervals, which are specified. The Guidance that accompanied the Act sought to address a number of weaknesses that had been identified in planning for children 'looked after'. It gave local authorities specific and detailed guidance, not simply regarding the role and function of planning and review processes, but on how the review meeting should be conducted.

The Guidance reflects the emphasis in the Children Act 1989 on ' partnership between parents, children and the responsible authority' (Vol. 4, 2.1). Unless it would prejudice the child's welfare, local authorities should work in partnership with parents and children. It is expected that where they are of sufficient age and understanding, 'children should participate actively in the decision-making process.' (Vol. 4, 2.10)

Young people should be consulted about their Care Plan and a written record be kept of this consultation, to inform the review meeting. In most authorities, consultation is achieved through the use of written consultation forms, which are sent out prior to the review meeting. The forms ask children specific questions related to their care and the plan for their future. The importance of this system of consultation was emphasised by the development and inclusion of consultation papers as part of the Department of Health materials I used.

Young people should also be involved in the review meeting. Subject to age and understanding, and except in those situations where attendance would not be in the their interests, it is expected that children will attend the review meeting: 'The attendance of the child and his parents will be the norm rather than the exception.' (Vol. 4, 3.15)

The Guidance and Regulations require that the review be chaired by an independent person and suggest that there is a clear agenda for each meeting. This should be circulated in advance to all those attending, including the child. In response, most authorities developed a standard agenda, and one is included in the review section of the Department of Health materials.

The Guidance also indicates who should be involved in the review meeting. This may include those

> with a legitimate interest in the child, where they have a contribution to make that indicates that they should take part in the discussions at the review meeting. The attendance of such people should always be discussed with the child before invitations are made. (Vol. 4, 3.17)

The young person should also be consulted about the date, time and venue of the meeting.

Young people's understanding of reviews

All of those children involved in the research completed and returned the consultation forms that were sent out to them. In addition they all attended, and spoke at, their review meetings. In most authorities this would be taken as evidence that they had been consulted and involved in the decision-making process.

However, the small body of research that exists on the involvement of children in the planning and reviewing process (Stein and Ellis 1983; Gardner 1985; Hodgson 1988; The Dolphin Project 1993; Grimshaw and Sinclair 1997) has raised doubts about the extent to which they actually participate in making plans for their future. The research project therefore looked in detail at the extent of children's involvement in the planning process.

The Children Act 1989 Guidance and Regulations viewed review meetings as 'part of a continuous planning process'. However, for those interviewed, planning was not a process but an event, and not always a welcome one. For many, the review was a formal and bureaucratic procedure that took place to meet the needs of social services, 'Its just people doing their job.' They were aware that a key purpose of review meetings was to monitor their progress, 'To check how we are getting on' and to make plans for their future; they all felt that reviews made decisions, although these decisions were not always the decisions that they wanted or expected.

The children interviewed experienced the planning process as static and this reflects the findings of other research studies, including that undertaken recently by Grimshaw and Sinclair (1997). The latter study found that decision-making was 'concentrated at the meeting'. As a consequence, the review meeting assumes a far greater significance in the planning process and the importance of involving young people becomes correspondingly more critical. If they are to influence decisions about their future, they must do so at the review meeting and so need to participate fully.

Consultation

For most of those children interviewed, consultation took place through the completion of the consultation forms sent out prior to the review. However, the consultation forms were viewed as boring and repetitive:

> That's the worst thing about reviews: you have to fill in forms and they're boring, because the words of the questions are the same as the questions you've already answered.

When discussing the consultation forms, several children were able to recall the exact wording of the questions, and the order in which they appear on the form. With three exceptions they completed the forms on their own. Those who completed the forms alone said that they tried to write as little as possible. 'We just write "Yes", "No", "Sometimes", "Don't know".' They gave several reasons for keeping their responses brief. Some spoke of the repetitive nature of the questions, which was underlined by the fact that they had completed the consultation forms several times before: 'We just do the same thing every year, write exactly the same thing about it.' Others said that they didn't know what to write. Some felt that the independent chairperson did not use the information they provided. For two siblings there was a very simple reason for keeping their answers brief:

> The last time we wrote loads about it, it took ages in the review. They kept bringing up the same thing up, 'Why did you write this?', 'Why did you write that?' and the review took ages.

Children who were supported in completing their forms, in two cases by their carer and in one by an independent helper arranged by their carer, said that they were helped to think about what they wanted the review to know and to express this in writing.

The information obtained through the consultation forms is limited, unless children are supported to complete them. The consultation forms on their own seem insufficient to enable individuals to express fully their views – without support they tended to provide only the briefest of answers. The consultation process, through the consultation forms alone, does not enable them to participate actively in the planning process.

Attendance

All of those interviewed attended their review meeting. Shemmings (1996) identified four ways in which children could be involved in meetings: to hear, to see, to speak and to be seen. These reflected the reasons given for attending meetings. The main reason for attendance was to hear what was being said – 'I didn't like them going to the review and talking about me and I couldn't hear what they were saying.'

Emphasis was placed on being listened to because, as we shall see, sometimes they felt that they were unable to influence the discussions which took place in the meeting. For some, the decision to attend was also influenced by the importance placed on the meeting by professionals: 'They go on and on at you about how important it [the meeting] is until you go.'

Organisation of the meeting

The Guidance and Regulations stress the importance of children's involvement in planning the meeting. Discussions with young people highlighted that they felt they had little say about when and where the meeting took place, or about who attended. Consultation on attendance focused on whether there was anyone the child wished to invite to the meeting. This was usually in addition to the list prepared by the social worker. Some said that they did not know all the participants at the meeting: 'There are people in my review that I don't even bloody know.'

Whilst others knew the *names* of all the individuals at the meeting, they were unclear about their role and why they attended: 'I don't know why Helen [Family Placement Link Worker] has to be there; but then I don't really know her job, so I don't know.' Sometimes they felt uncomfortable talking in front of 'people you don't even know', and many said that they talked less at the meeting because of this.

The way in which the date and time of the meeting was arranged provides a good example of their perceived lack of involvement in the planning process. One young person explained:

> At the end of the review everybody gets their diary out to arrange the next meeting. But I don't have a diary so nobody asks me.

Although the child is present at the meeting, and is 'technically' included in the question posed, the question is really directed to the adults and, hence, her or his involvement can be passive.

The scheduling of review meetings in advance also highlighted the tensions between the priorities of adults and children. Most young people do not plan their lives six months in advance. As a result, several reported that they had to miss what they considered to be more important events, because they clashed with the time of reviews arranged six months previously: 'I was chosen to play for the school team but I couldn't because they told me that the review was more important.' The lack of flexibility meant that some young people attended their meetings under sufferance and, thus, the likelihood that they could make a positive contribution was reduced.

For all of those interviewed, the review took place where they lived: 13 were happy with this arrangement; 2 felt uncomfortable that their reviews were held at their carers' homes. These two were concerned that it was difficult for their parents to hear about their progress, in the home of the people who were looking after them. This reflected the concerns that some children had about their parents, which often preoccupied them during the meeting.

Young people's involvement in the meeting

Most had a clear perception of the meeting as being run by and for the adults. They felt that the purpose of the meeting was to talk *about*, rather than *to,* them. The adults at the meeting 'talk very much among themselves'. Some felt that adults deliberately used language and concepts that excluded them: 'They try to talk over your head.' Even when they could contribute, it was limited by the fact that often questions about the child were directed at other adults. Consequently most felt overlooked and excluded for much of the meeting: 'It's everybody talking about us and we were just left in a dark corner and were not asked.' Several also felt that their contributions were listened to but not heard, and that to make their point heard they had to 'kick up a fuss'. This was often interpreted by the adults as difficult or delinquent behaviour, and most young people felt that the efforts they had to go to register their views 'wasn't worth the hassle'.

The view of the meeting as bureaucratic and adult-focused was increased by the use of standard agendas. As with the consultation forms, many children were able list the sequence of topics: 'They work through their list. Easy ones [subjects] at the beginning, hard ones at the bottom . . . . stressed out by the end.' As a result, they described having to sit through much of the meeting knowing that a difficult subject was going to come up, increasing their perception of the meeting as 'really stressful'. Many said that they were unable to concentrate on the other parts of the meeting because of their anxiety about more difficult areas. The use of standard agendas also meant that by the time the subject was raised the child had either forgotten any point they wished to make, or they felt that the atmosphere had become too stressful to speak.

Children said that leaving more complex or difficult issues until the end of the meeting meant that there was insufficient time to address them properly: 'It's like when you're running a race, you don't put your best runner on last.' As a result, they were faced with the option of a rushed discussion or having the meeting extended, neither of which was satisfactory to them. The average time for a review meeting was an hour and a half, although most told the researcher about meetings of two hours or longer; in one case it lasted four hours. The longer the meeting went on, the less they felt able to contribute: 'I start to listen at the beginning but as they get towards the end I just automatically switch off.'

Those interviewed found the review meetings stressful, for which there was a combination of reasons. Most felt inhibited in the presence of so many adults: 'They're all around you. It's you and them, so it's not very easy.' The presence of both parents and carers in the same venue was usually experienced as difficult. Young people had to manage their contributions in order to avoid upsetting anyone:

> I feel that I'm stuck in the middle and I have to say one thing to someone and say a different thing to someone else, and I end up playing one person against the other and everyone ends up getting angry with me.

To manage the stress they experienced, most children limited their contribution to answering questions:

> Everybody asks you questions. You don't know what to say, you don't know what they want to hear – I usually just sit there and listen to it all and when I get asked a question, depending on the question I'll just say 'Yes' or 'No'. If I get asked a detailed question, that also gets a 'Yes or 'No' answer as I don't want the reviews to go on.

For many children, the emphasis was often on keeping the meeting as short as possible, rather than making an effective contribution. Indeed, for a significant number this was a very good reason for not making a contribution.

For the children, the presence of so many adults, some of whom they may be in conflict with and others of whom they are anxious not to offend, in a meeting where they were the centre of attention proved to be extremely stressful: 'I just really want to get out as quickly as possible. I'm not really interested in the review.'

Conclusion

All of the young people interviewed completed consultation forms and attended their review. They all made a verbal contribution at the meeting. Their involvement in the planning process is limited by the concentration of decision-making at the review meeting. The review meeting is experienced as 'stressful' and 'boring'. The Department of Health materials I used in the study can improve the quality of information available to safeguard and promote the welfare of young people 'looked after'. However, the planning process itself, and review meetings in particular, need to be structured in ways that enable young people to participate actively, in order to ensure that plans made for their future are informed by their views.

References

Department of Health (1995) *Looking After Children.* London: HMSO.

The Dolphin Project, (1993) *Answering back: A report by young people on the Children Act 1989.* Southampton: Department of Social Work Studies, University of Southampton.

Gardner, R. (1985) *Child Care Reviews*. London: National Children's Bureau.

Grimshaw, R. and Sinclair, R. (1997) *Planning to Care: Regulation, Procedure and Practice under the Children Act 1989*. London: National Children's Bureau.

Hodgson, D. (1988) 'Participation not principles', *Social Services Insight*, 3, 30, pp. 20–1.

Shemmings, D. (1996) *Involving Children in Child Protection Conferences*, Social Work Monographs, No.152. Norwich: University of East Anglia.

Stein, M. and Ellis, S. (1983) *Gissa Say: Reviews and Young People in Care*. London: National Association of Young People in Care.

CHAPTER 7

ATTACHMENT THEORY
David Howe

Human beings are social beings. Our ability to cope with other people as friends, lovers, partners, parents, family members, neighbours and fellow workers is a measure of our social competence. People who are unable to function effectively in their relationships with others fail both personally and socially. And if the failure is marked, the experience of ineffective relationships spills beyond personal feelings of dissatisfaction to concerns of a more social and political nature. Men who are violent towards partners, fathers who abuse daughters, mothers who neglect babies, families who impair children's development, children who bully and attack peers, and pupils who disrupt classes and school life become of social concern, political interest and eventually statutory significance. It therefore matters a great deal how children become 'socially competent'.

We learn about relationships by being in relationships. Children learn to understand other people as they struggle to make sense of themselves and those around them. Indeed, the development of social understanding requires children to make sense of the self, other people, and the relationship between them. They can only do this by being in close, significant relationships themselves. To be an effective partner in a close relationship, children – particularly babies – need to make sense of the other person: 'What are they thinking, feeling, doing, intending, planning, wanting?' If the child is to participate physically, psychologically and socially, it is imperative that she or he understands what is going on in family life in general and intimate, caring relationships in particular (Dunn 1993).

However, the *quality* of these intimate and important relationships will profoundly affect children's ability to develop skilled and sensitive 'social understanding'. In turn, the quality of children's social understanding determines their level of social competence. It is clear, then, that children's social and interpersonal abilities develop within the relationships in which they find themselves and that the quality of these relationships is of major importance in affecting personality, emotional well-being and behaviour. The more adverse people's relationship history, the less strong and effective will they be in their interpersonal life. Rutter (1991) believes that:

> What has stood the test of time most of all has been the proposition that the qualities of parent–child relationships constitute a central aspect of parenting, that the development of social relationships occupies a crucial role in personality growth, and that abnormalities in relationships are important in many types of psychopathology.

Attachment theory – defined in its broader sense as a theory of the development of personality, emotional experience and behavioural styles within the context of close relationships – offers a powerful framework in which to understand people as partners, parents and creators of family life (Howe 1995). The pioneering and highly influential work of John Bowlby underpins all recent developments in attachment theory and the interested reader is well advised to turn to his writings (for example, Bowlby 1979 and 1988).

If we are to understand and work with children effectively and appropriately, we need to see the world from their point of view, both emotionally and cognitively. We need to be able to make sense of their thoughts and feelings within the social context in which they find themselves. Children have to function and survive in a range of emotional environments. The more adverse a child's social environment, the more difficult it will be for that child to develop a coherent sense of self. The world of other people becomes increasingly difficult to understand and handle. For the child in adversity, the result is distressed, disturbed and demanding behaviour. It is at this point that parents need help and welfare agents are called in.

Attachment theory and developmental perspectives in general provide coherent, well researched and elegantly argued ideas about the feelings, behaviours and psychological strategies we all use in our dealings with others, particularly if those others are our partners, parents or children. Although it is a theory that throws a bright light on the conditions and experiences of childhood, attachment theory also helps us understand adult personalities and behaviours too: 'Intimate attachments to other human beings are the hub around which a person's life revolves . . . .' (Bowlby 1988). Parents are the people most likely to provide children with their early, close relationship experiences. Attachment theory explores how the qualities of a child's relationship with a care giver transform into an individual characteristic of that child. Therefore, if we are to understand the quality of that child's developmental environment we also have to understand the parents, their personalities and the kinds of relationship they generate with each other and their children. If the social outside influences the child's psychological inside, we need to pay careful attention to the quality of the relationship between the two.

Attachment behaviour

Attachment behaviour is a biological response designed to ensure that babies can get into close, protective relationships. They need to get into such relationships at times of danger and anxiety. They also need to be in close relationship with their prime care givers in order to develop social understanding, interpersonal competence and language. By the time they are one year old, most children have established strong *selective attachments* to one or more adults or older children.

Attachment behaviours are triggered when children experience stress or anxiety. At such times, children seek out their attachment figure. This person is experienced as a 'secure base' – a place of safety and comfort. When children are not anxious or in need of comfort, they are free to explore and learn about the environment – of things and other people. It follows that children who experience a lot of anxiety have less time and emotional energy to explore and become socially adept. Securely attached children talk, play and explore more in their parent's company. They show a good deal of independence. Children who are insecurely attached to their parents are less relaxed, even when their parents are present. They do not play so much and are less able or inclined to play with other children.

Coping with loss and separation

Anxiety is a biologically normal reaction when we feel vulnerable or exposed, confused or uncertain. Our attachment figure provides us with a relationship that potentially reduces anxiety, confirms our personal importance and boosts feelings of self-worth. One of the most distressing experiences for a child is to be separated from or lose her or his attachment figure. The child's anxiety level is raised but the 'secure base' – the attachment figure herself or himself – is unavailable as a source of comfort. The normal reaction to such an experience is for the child to cry and protest vigorously. If the loss continues (say, the mother goes into hospital), the child goes into a stage of withdrawal and apathy. Nothing seems to interest the child and, should the separation continue, a final stage is reached in which she or he appears detached. The usual routines of life are resumed, but they are pursued mechanically. If the separation is prolonged, upon reunion the child will show an understandable mixture of relief, crying, anger, resentment and clinginess before the relationship finally returns to normal.

The occasional experience of loss or separation causes most children only temporary upset. No long-term damage is done. But for children who experience major separations and loss on a regular basis, the psychological demands are much greater and far tougher. It means that the attachment figure is not only the cause of the anxiety but is also not available as a source of comfort and reassurance. The emotional challenge for the child is how to cope with repeated and frightening surges of anxiety in the absence of a reliable or predictable attachment figure. These experiences can be handled in the short term but, as we shall see, there is a long-term and heavy psychological price to be paid. Moreover, it is not just the physical absence of the parent that is experienced as a loss or separation. Just as disturbing are parental indifference, emotional unavailability, and threats of abandonment or suicide. The messages implied in these behaviours are that the parent cannot be relied upon, the child is the cause of the loss, and the child is insufficiently loveable or worthwhile in the eyes of the care giver for her or him to guarantee remaining in the relationship. If the parent is the cause of the stress, the child is left psychologically alone to deal with the full impact of the anxiety.

Anxiety that cannot be reduced by attachment behaviour still has to be dealt with psychologically. Ways of trying to adjust to anxiety are known as the defence mechanisms (see Chapter 9).

> If the attachment figure is the cause of the anxiety, children simultaneously experience yearning for and anger with their care giver. Emotionally they will want to be close to their attachment figure and yet at the same time they will want to be rid of him or her because that person is also the cause of the pain and hurt. (Howe 1996)

Attachment classification system

Researchers and clinicians who have studied interactions between parents and their children have observed that the type of relationships they form depend on the parent's physical and emotional availability, sensitivity, reliability, predictability, responsiveness, level of interest and level of concern. Children who experience their attachment figures as usually available and responsive feel *secure*. Those who do not experience their attachment figures as reliably available and responsive feel varying degrees of *insecurity*.

Each type of relationship produces its own anxieties for, and psychological demands on, the child. In turn, each emotional relationship produces its own pattern of attachment. Mary Ainsworth worked with many of Bowlby's ideas and was the first to formulate an attachment classification system (Ainsworth *et al* 1978). Others have added to and refined the original classification, but the basic framework remains in good shape and of great relevance to social workers and other child welfare workers.

Including an extra category of 'non-attachment', we might recognise five types of attachment experience. Each type represents a certain kind of emotional relationship within which a child has to make particular kinds of psychological adjustment if she or he is to cope and survive. We have already said that aspects of the child's personality and ability to develop social understanding and competence form within these important relationships. Natural temperaments and degrees of resilience will certainly modify these outcomes, but the classification remains extremely useful in helping child care workers understand children's emotional experiences and behaviour. The theory insists that many features of our personality and emotional life form within the history of our relationships with others. Therefore, the different patterns of attachment lead to particular personality and relationship styles. The five types of attachment experience are:

1. Secure attachments.
2. Insecure attachments: ambivalent/resistant types.
3. Insecure attachments: avoidant types.
4. Insecure attachments: disorganised/disoriented types.
5. Non-attachments.

Secure attachments

Parental care within this pattern is generally loving, responsive, predictable and consistent. There is a sensitivity to children's needs, thoughts and feelings. Communication between care givers and children is rich and reciprocal. There is mutual interest and concern in the mental state of the other. Within such relationships children can learn about both themselves and social relationships. They develop feelings of self-worth, social relevance and competence. Other people are seen as trustworthy and available. Although distress is experienced when 'secure' babies are separated from their attachment figures, upon reunion they are comforted and soon settle. These children are usually sociable and well liked by their peers. They cope reasonably well with the conflicts, upsets and frustrations of everyday social life. To this extent, secure children understand and recognise the nature of their own as well as other people's feelings and so they cope well and appropriately with social relationships.

Ambivalent/resistant attachments

When parental care is inconsistent and unpredictable, children begin to experience increasing levels of anxiety. They are never quite sure of who they are and where they are in the context of these close and important relationships. The problem is one of neglect and insensitivity rather than hostility. Parents often fail to empathise with their children's moods, needs and feelings. Therefore, there is a lack of emotional synchrony and reciprocity. Misunderstandings and frustrations become increasingly common. Children are stimulated when they feel lethargic; not fed when they are hungry; blamed when they are innocent. Parents tend to respond to the child when they, as the care giver, need the child rather than when the child needs them. The effect of such care giving is to increase the child's distress and dependence. To this extent, children feel that the world of other people is hard to fathom and impervious to their influence and control. Love comes and goes in an entirely unpredictable manner. This generates a fretful, constant anxiety. Children become attention-seeking. They create drama and trouble in an attempt to keep other people involved and interested. Feelings are acted out.

Children in these kinds of relationship do not cope well with separation. They become highly distressed and are difficult to calm on reunion. They cling to their attachment figure in an attempt to stop them disappearing again, but they are also angry with them for causing them so much pain and distress. '*Ambivalent* children both demand parental attention and angrily *resist* it at the same time. They can never quite trust their parents. The fear of separation or being abandoned is ever present' (Howe 1996). Of course, the difficult and demanding behaviour that such relationships produce only makes matters worse, as exasperated parents continue to threaten dire consequences if the child carries on being a 'handful'.

Insensitive and inconsistent care is interpreted by children to mean that they are ineffective in securing love and sustaining comforting relationships. Their conclusion might be that not only are they unworthy of love but they might be unlovable. This is deeply painful. It undermines self-esteem as well as self-confidence. Thus, there is a need for closeness but a constant anxiety that the relationship might not last. Such feelings provoke jealousy, conflict and possessiveness. Children, indeed adults who have grown up in such relationships, are racked by insecurity. There is a reluctance to let go of relationships and yet a resentment and fear that they may be lost at any time. This gives rise to constant tension and conflict. On the surface, these children are sociable – even desperate to be liked by and involved with their peers. But they lack the balance and skill to keep relationships on an even keel. They ask too much of friendships and other children quickly tire of their demands and inability to let go or know when to stop. They are more likely to be bullied than be bullies.

Avoidant attachments

Whereas the attachment figures of resistant children do show feelings of love, albeit erratically, children who develop avoidant patterns of attachment have parents who are either indifferent, hostile or even rejecting of them. Although these parents may respond reasonably well when their child is content, they back off when she or he is distressed and needs closeness and attention. Children soon learn that there is little chance of comfort or concern being offered when they feel anxious or upset. The whining, clinging, complaining behaviour of the resistant child serves no purpose in these colder kinds of relationship. Parents encourage independence and de-emphasise dependency. When separated from their parents, these children show few signs of distress. Upon reunion, the children either ignore or avoid their attachment figure. They show little discrimination with whom they interact. There is no trust in, or reliance on, the adult world. Closeness to other people seems only to bring rejection and rebuff, pain and disappointment, and so they are better avoided. It seems better to become emotionally self-reliant, independent and self-contained. Feelings are suppressed. The conclusion must be that such hostility and rejection mean that the self is unlovable or even bad. Self-esteem is very poor.

Lack of emotional involvement and mutually satisfying relationships mean that these children find it very hard to understand and deal with their feelings. Conflict, anxiety and frustration are not handled well and can often lead to anger and aggression. Having had little experience of warmth and reciprocity in close relationships, empathy and interest in the feelings of others is low. The needs of other people are either not understood or ignored. These may not be popular children. They may bully and try to get their way through physical force rather than social skill.

Disorganised/disoriented attachments

It was recognised by some researchers and clinicians (for example, Main 1991) that many children who had suffered physical abuse and maltreatment seemed to show a confused mixture of resistant and avoidant patterns of attachment. The parent may not be wholly hostile or rejecting but there are times when they are dangerous and very frightening to the child. Relationships of this kind produce *disorganised and disturbed* attachment patterns, in which the violent parent's behaviour causes the child's anxiety. Anxiety normally triggers attachment behaviour in which the child approaches the parent for comfort. But in these cases, the attachment figure is the cause of the anxiety and so to approach her or him actually raises the level of anxiety. This poses an irresolvable conflict for such children. They find themselves wanting both to *approach* and to *avoid* the attachment figure at the same time. The result is that they either physically or emotionally 'freeze'. They remain emotionally confused and agitated in the presence of their care givers. This confusion extends to their dealings with other people. Distress and undirected, restless, agitated behaviour is often the result when children find themselves in close relationships. They do not know how to seek comfort nor do they seem to know how to respond to other people's warmth and concern. There is a general air of helplessness and disorientation. They appear as disturbed, socially isolated children.

Non-attachments

Although it is rare today for babies not to have had the opportunity to develop a *selective* attachment, it has been the case (and may still be the case in some overseas orphanages) that children raised in large residential nurseries have often failed to find an attachment figure. The nature of their social environment has meant that it has not been possible for them to form close *affectional bonds* (Bowlby 1979) with other people. Their physical care may have been good but their emotional needs were poorly met. Such children are indiscriminate in their willingness to relate to others: as long as people are able to meet their current need, they will do. Loss and separation cause no apparent distress. But without the benefit of a close, reciprocal, mutually sensitive relationship, these children find it difficult to recognise and deal with their needs and emotions. Their ability to understand themselves, others and the relationship between them is very poorly developed. Socially, these are inept children who have many, fleeting friendships but fail to sustain long-term relationships. They are easily frustrated, quick to temper, lacking in empathy and impulsive. The only time that social workers might meet such children in the UK is when parents are adopting a child who has been brought up in a large residential institution in a country that has suffered considerable social upheaval as a result of war, famine or poverty.

Understanding children in the context of their relationship with others

The simple fivefold framework of attachment patterns encourages workers to try to understand children, their emotions and behaviour in terms of the *quality* and *character* of the close social relationships in which they find themselves. Within each pattern there is basic defensive strategy being used by the child as she or he tries to cope with the anxieties that social life inevitably generates (Fahlberg 1994). In secure attachments children *move positively towards* their attachment figures as a potential resource; resistant children *move towards but against* their care givers; avoidant children *move away from* their attachment figures; and disoriented children *stand still* in the face of distress and anxiety. Each of these defensive strategies makes perfect sense within the context of the relationship. Under the circumstances, they can be seen as adaptive psychological responses. But beyond the attachment relationship and into adult life, the more insecure patterns provide the child with less flexibility and fewer skills when dealing with the self and other people. By understanding children's emotional history and its impact on personality and behaviour, child care practitioners may increase their own sensitivity, accuracy and effectiveness when working with children in need (Howe *et al,* forthcoming).

References

Ainsworth, M. D. S., Blehar, M. C., Waters, E. and Wall, S. (1978) *Patterns of Attachment.* New Jersey, NJ.: Erlbaum.

Bowlby, J. (1979) *The Making and Breaking of Affectional Bonds.* London: Tavistock.

Bowlby, J. (1988) *A Secure Base.* London: Routledge, p. 442.

Dunn, J. (1993) *Young Children's Close Relationships: Beyond Attachment.* Newbury Park: Sage, p. 361.

Fahlberg, V. (1994) *A Child's Journey Through Placement.* London: BAAF.

Howe, D. (1995) *Attachment Theory for Social Work Practice.* Basingstoke: Macmillan.

Howe, D. (1996) 'Attachment theory in child and family social work' in Howe, D. (ed.) *Attachment and Loss in Child and Family Social Work.* Aldershot: Avebury, p. 8, p. 11.

Howe, D., Brandon, M., Hinings, D. and Schofield, G. (forthcoming, 1999) *Attachment Theory, Child Maltreatment and Family Support: A Practice and Assessment Model.*

Main, M. (1991) 'Metacognitive knowledge, metacognitive monitoring, and singular (coherent) vs multiple (incoherent) model of attachment', pp 127–59, in Parkes, C. M., Stevenson-Hinde, J. and Marris, P. (eds) *Attachment Across the Life Cycle.* London: Tavistock/Routledge.

Rutter, M. (1991) 'A fresh look at maternal deprivation' in Bateson, P. (ed.) *The Development and Integration of Behaviour.* Cambridge: Cambridge University Press, p. 361.

CHAPTER 8

MAKING SENSE OF SEPARATION AND LOSS: THE CHILD'S EXPERIENCE
Gillian Schofield

Given that the principle of participation is an important part of good practice in relation to all our child clients, it is necessary to look closely at specific factors that have a part to play in affecting how children make sense of their family situation and the implications for social work practice in facilitating their participation. One such factor is children's experience of separation and loss, a theme that traditionally has aided our understanding of many children who are living in stressful circumstances and may be in need of help or protection.

Why might separation and loss affect a child so significantly? Why do such experiences need to be taken into account in the work that is done with children to enable them to be actively involved in family support and child protection work? Let us consider briefly some of the referrals that bring children to the attention of statutory or voluntary agencies: a child has become out-of-control at home and has started setting fires; a child is so distressed at school that she cannot concentrate on her work and appears to be both physically and emotionally neglected; a 12-year-old girl has talked of sexual abuse, is frequently absent from school and has been picked up by the police for prostitution; a boy refuses to change for PE and it is discovered that he has bruises on his back. For many such children, the history of concerns about significant harm will also reveal such factors as disrupted relationships with parents or step-parents, the death of a grandparent, perhaps frequent moves of house or school and possibly episodes of local authority accommodation in their early years. What we need to remember is that before the current referral, these children will have been trying to make sense of what is happening to them. This is an *emotional* and a *cognitive* process in which they will have attempted to understand why parents may be behaving in a particular way towards them (rather than towards a sibling perhaps) or why other children at school appear to have very different lives from them. Why do people leave or die? What is it about them as children that has deserved such a childhood or has even brought it about? What should they feel about the adults in their lives or about themselves? When children are trying to make sense of their lives, certain kinds of experiences will affect the internal narrative or framework within which they construct such explanations. Among these experiences, the experience of separation and loss in childhood will affect children's views of the world in quite profound ways and will therefore contribute significantly to the way in which children view themselves.

When concerns are raised in the professional network, professionals certainly need to understand what is happening in a factual sense in the family. However, if they are going to take the next step and enable the child to be actively involved in the work that goes on with the family and the decisions that are to be made, they need to get in touch with the child's construction of events, including both the cognitive version and the emotional consequences. Moreover, they need to be aware of cultural and ethnic differences in the way in which separation and loss are experienced and feelings about it expressed. Children who have communication difficulties or disabilities will also need to be given the opportunity to express their feelings in whatever ways are appropriate. Difficult and distressing past experiences should not limit the child's involvement but they do mean that workers have to be able to listen to all children, whatever their circumstances, in ways that take into account the complexity of their emotional lives. Understanding the child's experience of separation and loss will be an important part of that process.

When we consider the importance of separation in this context, it is important to take the following into account:

- Separation and loss are universal features of children's development.
- Some children find it hard to cope with such 'normal' experiences because of the specific family or social circumstances in which they find themselves.
- A number of children experience loss of a more radical kind, such as the death of a parent or repeated separations and losses of family members through family breakdown.
- Separation and loss may also be part of a child's experience of abuse and neglect.
- The intervention of agencies that become involved to help or protect because of concerns about a child may introduce additional burdens in terms of separation and loss if the child needs to be looked after by the local authority.

Each of these five separate but connected categories may have an impact on the child's perspective on their lives, their relationships and any decisions that affect them. Such factors must be understood fully by workers if they are going to help children to maximise their capacity to be involved as 'persons' rather than 'objects of concern' in the processes that affect them (Butler-Sloss 1988).

Separation and loss as part of normal development

From the early weeks of life, babies have to face the fact that the attention and care of their parent is only available intermittently. As Winnicott (1964) suggested, the 'good enough' parent makes herself or himself available to meet the child's needs for food and for comfort but there are inevitably points in time – brief separations – when the child begins to learn to wait. For the securely attached child, that waiting will be experienced as low in anxiety because the child can rely on the fact that the parent will appear before the child's need has become too desperate. For the insecurely attached child, such waiting periods may be full of anxiety. Out of this process comes the basis of the child's internal working model of self and others, which affects how subsequent separations and losses are experienced (although later experiences may affect this core capacity).

During childhood it is a necessary part of development that the child moves from total dependency to an increasing sense of autonomy. From the second year of life, children are negotiating their own identity by asserting themselves in relation to the adult world. In this context, all developmental gains are accompanied by the experience of loss. For example, as children learn to walk, they gain freedom but lose the right to be carried and cuddled. When children are developing normally, the gains outweigh the losses and they get their need to be cuddled met in other ways. In the first major experience of separation, which may be at playgroup or school, children learn that they can cope for longer periods of time without the presence of a parent or other family member. Securely attached children can manage their own anxiety or they can use other adults or children to obtain emotional support.

In the teenage years, children work towards a further significant stage of separation as they move into adult life. Even during this period, teenagers need a secure base in the form of reliable relationships in order to cope with the demands of adolescence.

Coping with separation and loss in adversity

If we think about this familiar pattern in childhood, it is apparent that there will be a range of experiences depending on family and social circumstances and that the negotiation of different stages will be less than smooth for many children. If parents are coping with several young children and living under stress in poor housing conditions, it will be considerably more difficult for them to be available, either physically or emotionally, to each child. Children are more likely to be left on their own if there is no telephone to ring the doctor or the benefits office and if there are no family members or friends living nearby. The majority of parents manage to provide a sense of security to their children even in these difficult circumstances, but if other factors are also present then the children's experiences may put their emotional security at risk. If parents are misusing drugs or alcohol, for example, the risk to the child is often greatest when a parent needs to leave the children on their own in order to get to a dealer or to get supplies of alcohol. In these more extreme circumstances, the children may find that parents provide not only less emotional and physical availability while present (because of drug or alcohol intoxication) but also that they have unpredictable periods of absence. If these experiences become a common feature of a child's life, then the immediate sense of distress is likely to build into a pattern of responses that affects the child's approach to any situation of separation. Just as the young baby develops internal working models based on experiences of predictable, close relationships, so children who persistently experience unpredictable separations and a failure of the normal 'holding environment' may live their entire lives in the fear that they will be separated and will not be able to cope.

Loss of attachment figures

We know that, when children experience the loss of a parent through death, the process of bereavement is likely to form a pattern similar to that experienced by adults. Children too can experience shock, denial, anger, bargaining, despair, and acceptance or integration (Kubler-Ross 1970). What we might think of as a healthy process of mourning is predicated to some extent on the idea that the child is fundamentally healthy emotionally and that the environment that surrounds the child is able to offer security and facilitate this move towards some form of resolution. For children who are already causing concern to professional agencies, the losses they experience may appear less traumatic than the death of a parent but the framework in which they experience losses, both psychologically and socially, is significantly more fragile. Children who live in chaotic households where the parental figures are constantly changing may have to adapt frequently to a pattern of brief relationships that begin and end in an apparently random way. When such relationships end, particularly if this is associated with domestic violence, children are left trying to make sense of the loss they have experienced. Having built up a picture of the now departed parent figure as the source of both security and anxiety, it is likely that the loss will provoke extremely confused and ambivalent feelings in the child.

Abuse and neglect

When this pattern of events occurs in the context of parenting, which may be neglectful or abusive, the child has a dual dilemma: making sense of the experience of poor parenting, and of loss. The fragile self-esteem that neglect and abuse of all kinds create means that making sense of loss increasingly becomes a process of self-blame. Although 'magical thinking' is often associated with young children, children of all ages who experience loss in this context are likely to blame themselves for the departure of their parent's partner or the financial destitution in which they find themselves. Children are unlikely to be able to mourn successfully the lost relationship and to move towards a sense of resolution.

Children in substitute care

For most children coming into contact with professional agencies, the aim will be to offer support in the child's own family. This focus arises from an acknowledgement that even children whose development has been impaired or who are at risk of significant harm may suffer further harm if they are exposed to separation or disruption in their close relationships and in their environment.

If children cannot be kept safe within their own families, it will be necessary for them to be offered the opportunity of a safe environment in substitute care. It is at this point that we need to be aware both of the circumstances in their family life, which will affect their experience of *this* separation, and of the ways in which this awareness can contribute to the work that the social worker is undertaking with the child.

Children who come into foster or residential care have to make sense of these events, just as they have had to make sense of other experiences of separation and loss. The first thing to bear in mind is that one of the functions of attachment figures is to provide a source of support in a stressful situation. In this particular situation the cause of the stress is the loss of the attachment figure, and the child may not know where to turn. The *quality of the attachment* will affect the nature of this experience. The securely attached child initially may experience great distress but is more likely to be able to build a level of trust with a carer and use that relationship to cope with the anxiety than an insecurely attached child, whose internal working model is likely to lead to distrust.

We need to be aware that children may also be experiencing the *loss of other significant relationships*. For the child whose source of security was an aunt or grandparent, or a large extended family, this loss may be as great as the loss of a parent and this may not be recognised if only parental contact is offered. Sibling relationships can be particularly important when there has been a shared experience of abuse or neglect, and separation in this context can leave all the children feeling disoriented and distressed. Friendships at school and relationships with teachers may also have become very important and may be lost.

Fahlberg (1994) has suggested that there are a number of ways in which children make sense of this separation and that each explanation has consequences for children's views of their situation and their emotional reaction to it:

- Children may think that they have been taken away from their parents or 'kidnapped'. This threatens their sense of confidence in their parents' power to protect them and leads to *heightened anxiety*.
- Children may fear that they have been *given away* by their parents. This means that they were not good enough and leads to feelings of *sadness and depression*.
- Children may believe that *they have caused* the loss of the parent by something they have done. This may lead the child to feel excessively *powerful and responsible* for subsequent events.

These explanations may occur whether the child is accommodated as a result of parents feeling unable to cope or when removed by a court order. In this sense it is the child's reality that needs to be grasped before the worker can engage the child in the process of assessment and helping.

Because there are links between *reactions to loss* and *reactions to abuse*, especially in terms of heightened levels of anxiety and certain kinds of regression, it is particularly important to distinguish between them in practice. Children who wet the bed or smear faeces in foster or residential care may be demonstrating behaviour which reflects deep-rooted disturbance arising from abuse or neglect; but they *may* be demonstrating a profound reaction to loss.

Age and developmental stages will also affect the impact on the child of admission to foster or residential care. If children are separated at a stage when they are already negotiating a process of increasing autonomy (such as the toddler, or the child starting at school, or the adolescent), then they are likely to regress or in some cases become too self-reliant. Teenagers may find it difficult to become attached to a new foster family at a stage when they are increasingly autonomous and looking to their peer group for relationships. Unfortunately, they will still be in need of a secure base to help them through a stressful situation, and this may be difficult to identify.

Implications for practice

Given the high levels of stress for children associated with separation and loss of all kinds, what are the implications for social workers with children in the field of family support and protection? Perhaps the most important element for workers to bear in mind is the fact that a child's wishes and feelings in these circumstances are never simple, any more than an adult's views on a complex situation would be. Most children want to be with their families but wish desperately for things to be different; when the child is at risk of significant harm, this is never a simple option. What characterises many situations is that children are *ambivalent*. If a child has experienced distress or pain in the family home, then respite care or foster care can bring relief. But for all the reasons cited above, separation is inherently anxiety-provoking and children can feel very torn between the options available to them. They may feel a strong sense of loyalty to parents and find it very hard to trust carers or social workers. When it comes to decision-making, children will need a great deal of help if these complex feelings are to be represented properly, whether by the child attending child protection conferences in person or through a social worker or advocate.

It has sometimes been argued that highly vulnerable children should be protected from the burden of involvement in the bureaucratic, formal and inherently stressful decision-making forums that characterise child protection. This seems to confuse *responsibility for decision-making*, which continues to rest with the professionals or the courts in consultation with the parents, with *participation*, which should be the right of all children. I would argue that children who have experienced anxiety around separation or abuse have often done so because of a sense of powerlessness in the face of adult behaviour. It is therefore essential that even very vulnerable children should begin to feel that their views matter and are taken into account. This does not necessarily mean that children will want to attend all meetings, but it does mean that they should be aware of the role that their wishes and feelings can play.

Although traumatic experiences should not be used to minimise the role of the child's wishes and feelings, such children will need time and sensitivity from workers. Sometimes workers believe they are protecting children by not raising painful issues, such as the unpredictable nature of a parent's mental illness. Often workers may be in effect *protecting themselves from children's grief*, but thereby they leave children without the information and the opportunity to express feelings and to check their fantasies against reality. As Jewett (1994) has put it: 'Even in peripherally involved adults, a child's loss strikes a deep chord, triggering strong feelings left over from past losses, separations, or rejections of their own.

Maintaining an emotional availability to the child will therefore require considerable support from colleagues and from supervision.

What is needed is a model of social work practice that incorporates both the skills required to help a child cope with experiences of separation and loss and the skills required to help a child participate in the process of assessment, helping and decision-making. These skills are in many ways compatible, although the child's emotional vulnerability and cognitive difficulty in making sense of loss will affect what might be seen as a basically straightforward process of helping the child 'make sense' of the available options and develop a view about them. Such skills will include the following:

- Observing children's behaviour and reactions to separation.
- Listening to children with respect and sensitivity.
- Giving the child clear information.
- Understanding and accepting the child's ambivalence.
- Building a relationship of trust.
- Empowering children to express their wishes and feelings.

Aldgate and Simmonds (1988) have suggested that:

> .... intervention designed to affect mediation of the negative effects of separation and loss must be based on a fundamental belief that separation involves a fear which needs to be mastered and loss involves grief which needs to be expressed.

Facilitating this process needs to take place alongside the work involved in enabling a child to participate. Children who feel involved, valued and listened to when decisions are made will be better able to make sense of even the most distressing situations of separation and loss. Children who are allowed to talk through their most deep-seated anxieties and fears will be better able to make sense of the options available to them. Such an integration is a necessary part of working with children and draws on basic social work principles, in which openness, honesty and respect for the child are central.

References

Aldgate, J. and Simmonds, J. (eds) (1988) *Direct Work with Children.* London: BAAF, p. 44.

Butler-Sloss, E. (1988) *The Report of the Inquiry into Child Abuse in Cleveland.* London: HMSO.

Fahlberg, V. (1994) *A Child's Journey Through Placement.* London: BAAF.

Jewett, C. (1994) *Helping Children Cope with Separation and Loss.* London: Batsford.

Kubler-Ross, E. (1970) *On Death and Dying.* London: Tavistock.

Winnicott, D. (1964) *The Child, the Family and the Outside World.* Harmondsworth: Penguin.

CHAPTER 9

DEFENCES AND ADAPTIVE RESPONSES
Judith Trowell

As human beings, we are constantly thinking and feeling – that is, our world is in large part preoccupied with our emotional and psychological state. The body is often ignored unless it is in pain or is cold, hungry or tired. Mental life is therefore very significant and can be seen as an interplay between the external world shared by us all, and the internal world, which is much more specific to the individual. Psychodynamically, the internal world is shaped by early experiences and innate factors including personality, genetic predisposition, current and past relationships, and life events such as trauma and loss. Attachment relationships are highly important in forming the structure – the scaffolding – within the internal world.

To live and to be alive involves conflict. The only time conflict is over is when one dies. The conflictual situation may be love or hate, like or dislike, generosity or greed, altruism or envy, activity or passivity, avoidance or aggression – that is, to do with feelings – or it may be the result of certain 'facts of life': male and female, parents and children, life and death. Differences can also give rise to conflict, certainly in the external world and therefore in ways that are only beginning to be understood in the internal world. These can include differences between concepts of 'able-bodied' and 'disabled', racial and cultural differences and sexual orientation, for example.

In order to manage these conflicts, the mind needs to maintain a mental state that can continue to function. Again, viewed psychodynamically, it is argued that within the internal world there are two main areas or divisions: the conscious and the unconscious. The conscious mind is aware of the external world and interacts; the unconscious mind has to contain and manage the very powerful feelings, longings, desires and thoughts that arise from 'inside' ourselves and that are provoked by what happens to us. In order for our conscious mind to be able to be reasonably clear and effective, any thoughts or feelings that are so conflictual that we feel threatened are consigned to the unconscious or, if they arise from within, are kept in the unconscious. The way this is done is through the defences. This capacity is one of our most impressive adaptive responses because it enables human beings to make their conflictual states manageable so that their functioning is kept relatively unimpaired.

Conflictual thoughts and feelings are experienced in the mind as fantasies, because the person in a state of conflict does not perceive the conflict as such but is consciously or unconsciously torn between differing and frequently incompatible wishes or fears. The richness of human mental life arises from this and can be seen as dreams, paintings, poetry, music, inventions, discoveries and all forms of creativity. Our creative capacity is another adaptive response.

Defences

As we grow, our means of dealing with conflict evolves. Early in life, feelings are very intense and there are basic ways of making these feelings manageable. Defences are available to us and we revert to them in times of stress, illness, trauma and crises. They are: splitting, denial, manic flight, magical thinking, projection and projective identification.

There is healthy and unhealthy (or pathological) *splitting* and *denial*, when feelings, thoughts and relationships are not seen as being of any importance, but then the person's functioning is left depleted and diminished and with no way of resolving the issue (this all takes place within the unconscious). If faced with a crisis, or, for example when a parent is faced with the demands of children, then a healthy splitting and denial of one's own needs and wishes can enable one to carry on and function. When a situation is unbearable, and the psychic pain threatens to be overwhelming, then *manic flight* (that is, to become excited, restless and somewhat omnipotent) may be a way of coping.

Magical thinking can be dangerous if the individual really believes thinking a thought makes it happen, but it is often part of our thinking – buying lottery tickets thinking we might win! Children are often deeply troubled by this, believing that *they* caused someone to die or their parents to split up because they had the thoughts. The child is then left feeling responsible.

Projection and *projective identification* are rather more complex as concepts but, nevertheless, are an important part of our capacity to communicate healthily and to eliminate unbearable feelings. They are also an unconscious mechanism that attempts to control significant others in our external world. The baby relies heavily on projection and projective identification. Feelings, sensations and very simple thoughts of hunger, distress, discomfort and loneliness in the baby are conveyed to the carer, who, hopefully, is available and receptive and then allows herself or himself to become aware of these communications. The baby communicates by projective identification and the carer introjects (or 'takes in') this unconscious communication. This message is then processed by the carer, who tries to sort out whether the hunger, distress or discomfort is her or his own or whether the baby, by its cry, body posture and non-verbal signals, is telling the carer something about herself or himself. The emotionally healthy carer can decide that it is the baby who is hungry and then sets about feeding the baby. This type of communication is repeated over and over and so the baby introjects an image of an 'other', who is responsive, thoughtful and in touch and who can manage painful and difficult thoughts and feelings. This provides the basis for trust and mental health.

But parents or carers may be confronted by this needy baby at a time when *they* feel needy, and may not be able to sort out whether it is the baby or themselves who is hungry and distressed; additionally, they may feel intruded upon and persecuted by the baby's communication. They might not respond, or they may respond angrily. The baby now introjects an 'other' who cannot think or feel (perhaps the carer is depressed and preoccupied) or an 'other' who is rejecting (perhaps the carer did not want the baby, or the baby resembles a hated person).

This form of unconscious communication continues throughout life, but hopefully more verbal and more conscious communication predominates. Even so, in stressful situations between family members or between partners this form of managing unmanageable thoughts and feelings is used. Often, professionals entering family systems can be caught up in, and blown off course by, such powerful feelings.

Many other defence mechanisms can be seen as developments of projective identification, but it is useful to be aware of the different processes in order to understand how we and those around us are functioning. *Displacement* is when thoughts or feelings are moved from the self or one person onto another, who then can be attacked or admired. *Identification* with the aggressor is a means of coping with feeling small, powerless and vulnerable, for example when an abused child in adolescence later becomes a bully or an abuser.

When conflicts in the external world, or those arising from the internal world, become too intense, one way of managing is with *repression*: conscious thoughts and feelings enter the unconscious and are held there 'forgotten'. However, this can be very difficult to maintain if the fantasies associated with the accompanying thoughts and feelings demand immediate expression and so, quite often, they emerge into conscious awareness or as precipitate actions that surprise the individual (such as an intense outburst of rage provoked by quite a small irritating incident).

Regression comes into action whenever conflicting thoughts or feelings are so intense that one's typical skills and competences disappear, leaving the individual drawing on much earlier behavioural patterns. This happens quite often with children who start to soil and wet again when a new baby arrives, thereby taking most of the parents' attention, or the adult who loses her or his job and becomes very vulnerable, demanding and dependent on other family's members.

When a conflict has not been resolved adequately, or when the outcome is unsatisfactory, one way is to engage in repetitive compulsion. Unconsciously the individual repeats the same situation in an attempt to find a better outcome. The girl who was physically abused may repeat the likelihood of abuse in her adult relationships, by 'choosing' potentially violent partners. There is an unconscious need to be able to love enough and be loved enough, this time to overcome the violence and gain mastery and self-esteem – but all too frequently it is not possible and violence is repeated.

Undoing is an interesting way of managing conflict. Having done something good, bad or neutral, the individual experiences such an inner conflict that they need either to do the opposite, or try and render what was first done as null and void in an almost magical way. Many rituals and obsessions can be understood in this way – for example, unconscious desires to cause chaos, make a mess, and destroy can be dealt with by constant tidying up and cleaning.

Disavowal can be understood as a form of splitting, so that two incompatible ideas are held at the same time and, thus, external reality is denied. It is frequent in small children but can be problematic in adults. A person who has finally agreed that they have sexually abused a child, may have extensive evidence of the duration of abuse but may still try and maintain either that they didn't do it, or, that if they did it then it was a mistake, a one-off incident which will never happen again. They may be lying, but sometimes it is disavowal and there are two incompatible ideas in their minds – 'I did it', 'I didn't do it' – because to face what they have done is unbelievable and is pushed into their unconscious.

Reparation is a healthier means of trying to make things better. Attempts are made to try and repair or restore the damage done; but, in true reparation, this has to mean accepting guilt.

Guilt that is unconscious, because it is too intense, can lead to *manic reparation*, namely attempts to make better by magic, or to 'rub out' without really acknowledging the pain and distress. *Sublimation* is rather different. It is a way of redirecting impulses into activity that is socially approved. Individuals who choose careers in caring for children may have found a solution to the problem of needing to have others dependent on them. A young person who experiences aggressive feelings may find satisfaction where controlled aggression is an essential ingredient of the new job.

It can be seen that defences are neither good nor bad in themselves, but simply devices to maintain an emotional equilibrium. It is only when defences become fixed and inflexible and maintaining them consumes so much psychological energy that aspects of the real world are filtered out. In this situation an individual can neither see people nor events realistically.

Almost without exception, social workers deal with young people who are in a heightened sense of anxiety, with their defences aroused. It makes sense therefore to be aware of how a child characteristically reacts to stress, what defences are used and how constructive these are in managing and solving problems. Many children have difficulties that are clearly not of their own making. Yet at other times the way they go about their lives can seem self-destructive and designed to alienate – or test out – potentially helpful people. Such young people can challenge the idea social workers have of themselves as helpful. Without defending poor practice, these children deny that they have ever received assurance and support and frequently are disparaging about their social workers.

Unless social workers understand the nature of defence mechanisms, any assessment is likely to be partial and ways of helping less finely tuned. As a rule of thumb, anybody – younger or older – who makes heavy use of defence mechanisms needs supportive help initially. This is, of course, the opposite of the natural impulse of a helper to insist that someone recognises a problem and faces up to its likely cause. However, the skilled worker will not subject a young person to more anxiety than can constructively be tolerated and will be aware of defences that are essential to their emotional economy. To do otherwise is likely to make a young person more resistant to change and less inclined to reason.

Conclusion

Adaptive responses lead to a capacity for empathy, to altruism and ultimately to maturity. They increase one's capacity to let go, whether this is to give one's child independence or 'let go' a thought, a picture, a book, an invention or an idea. This is the final aim of the adaptive responses that the defences have developed to facilitate: when conflicts have been managed sufficiently well to enable individuals to fulfil their potential.

CHAPTER 10

EMOTIONAL AND COGNITIVE DEVELOPMENT
Diana Hinings

Knowledge of how children grow and develop is an essential strand in the repertoire of social workers engaged in the complex job of helping children and their families. This, of course, is not enough on its own; imagination and sensitivity in relation to the child's experience are equally important. However, the tasks that social workers undertake, such as assessing a child's well-being, deciding how her or his needs can best be met, and talking to children, all require an understanding of children at each age and stage as they grow. Two points need to be made at the outset. First, that children exist as physical, social, emotional and cognitive beings. Considering emotional and cognitive development separately is merely a convenient device. Secondly, the way in which a child grows and develops, and the adult she or he subsequently becomes, is a result of a unique cocktail – a mix of genetic endowment (including personality traits) and the social circumstances into which the child is born. It is different for every child, even for those born to the same parents in a family that stays together.

This chapter is concerned with the patterns and sequences of children's emotional and cognitive development. Knowledge about emotion and cognition comes from three main sources. There are the theorists such as Melanie Klein (1986) and Erik Erikson (1959) who propose models for understanding emotional life. For example, how can we understand how an infant feels who has been left to cry in the cot for half an hour? The child is red-faced, sweating and distressed; Klein asserts that the child feels that the outside world is hostile and is overwhelmed with feelings of rage and anxiety. Like Klein, Erickson regards the child's relationship with the outside world as crucial to future development and sees this neglect of the child's needs as leading to a sense of distrust. Such a child will, he believes, lack confidence and self-esteem and be reluctant to explore a seemingly unresponsive environment.

The second source of knowledge comes from empirical research. Developmental psychologists have, in the last decade, generated an explosion of knowledge about the cognitive capacities of very young infants and their social responsiveness.

A third contribution to knowledge comes from observation of infants and young children in their ordinary living situation. The role of the observer is often uncomfortable because the tensions and anxieties experienced in the intimate exchanges between a small child and a parent can be 'caught' by the observer. Observation is used also as a technique in the training of psychotherapists and social workers, both to provide insights into the emotional life of pre-verbal children and as preparation for tolerating difficult feelings.

Infancy

Donald Winnicott (1971), a paediatrician and psychoanalyst, wrote that 'there is no such thing as a baby'. He was making the point that an infant cannot grow and develop in isolation but only in the context of a relationship with a nurturing person. Babies who are reared in institutions do not thrive, even though they receive an adequate amount of food and physical care. Similarly, children who experience many different carers, maybe moving from one situation to another, suffer delayed development and emotional disturbance. Sadly, when the children eventually arrive at a setting in which they can remain, they have difficulty in responding to the love and care that is offered. Thus, it seems that a relationship with a carer who is both reliably available and responsive and committed to the child is a necessary condition for growth and development into a socially competent human being. Lack of such a relationship is a powerful predictor of future emotional and social difficulties and consequent unrealised potential.

Whilst a connection between the quality of a child's early relationships and subsequent development is accepted by all but the most sceptical, exactly how this works is harder to document. This is where the theorists enter the frame and take over from the researchers. For the very young baby, the relationship with the caring person is her or his entire environment. The baby has no options or choices. If that relationship fails the infant, then the world is an unpredictable and frustrating place. Professionals who care for disturbed children know that it is not unusual for a 9- or 10-year-old child to be curiously unaware of their own body sensations. The child may wear a thick jumper on a hot day and be in obvious discomfort, but have no idea that s/he would feel better if s/he took it off. S/he may stay in a swimming pool until s/he is shivering but deny that s/he feels cold. These are children who have not experienced a rhythm of reliable care from an early age and as a result they lack the ability to make sense of their experience.

Vera Fahlberg (1994), a psychiatrist who works with disturbed children, suggests that parents who seek advice about how to respond to their young infants should be advised to ask themselves 'What will help my child to trust me?' In a warm and trusting climate the infant's inborn social, physical and intellectual capacity develops and her or his parents applaud and support each achievement. By the age of twelve months, an infant has achieved a great deal; about 50 per cent of babies are walking and all except those who have a disability are mobile. They understand 'No' and other simple commands and shout to attract attention. It has been said that infants are constantly faced with situations that either violate or confirm their expectations and they now register a range of emotions in the course of a day's explorations. At some time between the ages of seven and nine months, a baby makes clear a preference for her or his carers over everyone else. This excludes friends and relatives who may visit frequently but who still are treated, at least initially, as strangers. From this point the presence of the carer is needed for the child to be relaxed and comfortable enough to play and explore.

From toddler to schoolchild

From the time a child recognises the primary carer, s/he is dependent on her or his presence in order to feel secure. If separated, the child reacts with vigorous protest and the ordinary activities of exploration and being 'into everything' come to a halt. Paradoxically, a child needs the continuing availability of the person to whom s/he is most attached in order to develop a sense of self as a separate person. This attachment provides a 'secure base' until the child is old enough to have the security of the carer as 'an inner certainty as well as an outer predictability'. This is achieved around the age of 3 years old, when the child can more easily tolerate short separations from carers.

As well as emotional gains, the toddler is becoming highly mobile and it seems that each week s/he can reach a new shelf or open a new cupboard that was previously safe from her or his attentions. Children are keen to test their developing strength and to do things unaided. Their reaction to failure or someone taking over the job is usually angry frustration. Fahlberg advises parents to ask the question 'What will make my child feel competent?' when dealing with a wilful toddler.

Children of this age are preoccupied by whether things are big or small and younger siblings are tolerated because of their inferior size. Adults intuitively collude with the toddler who claims 'I'm a big girl, I did it all myself!' Toddlers who are teased or belittled easily collapse into tears of rage and their drive for self-reliance is likely to be dented. Most parents find that some adaptations to the house are necessary in order to reduce the need for vigilance; precious ornaments are moved and staircases barred.

The child's emerging sense of self begins with an awareness of the distinction between 'me' and 'not me'. Many children have a treasured object, sometimes a soft toy or a blanket, to which they are greatly attached and which has to be with them at all times. Winnicott identifies this as the first 'not me' object. Seen in these terms, the importance of a battered teddy bear makes more sense! At a time when toddlers are developing a sense of being separate from their carer, their thinking is egocentric. They see events and people only in relation to themselves. They do, however, have some ability to understand emotions and may attempt to comfort another child who is upset. Indeed, siblings in their home environment as young as 14 to 16 months may do this. But, at the same time as a toddler may show admirable concern for another child, at other times s/he may remove a desired toy from another child with whatever force is necessary.

Toddlers have a short attention span. This is irritating if the child tires of the idea of playing in the paddling pool the minute it has been filled with water but a bonus when a child can be easily diverted from an undesirable activity. Their moods, both positive and negative, are short-lived. As the child moves nearer to school age, her or his personality becomes more organised and competence increases. Movements are more graceful and language is developed so that s/he sounds more like an adult. Most importantly, s/he can cope more easily in the absence of a parent. The waking hours are spent in play and, as Erikson observed, 'play is a child's work'. Pre-school children spend most of their time in small, manageable groups – their family or playgroup. They are increasingly acute observers in relation to their surroundings, but there is often a gap between what is perceived and what is understood. At this age the child frequently will fabricate an explanation which s/he feels fits the facts. This is particularly the case in relation to sex and reproduction! Children's thinking at this stage is 'magical': they believe that they cause events to happen by thinking about them. They also believe that other people have these frightening powers as well. Bowlby (1979) reminds us that children fear threats of abandonment more than threats of loss of love. A parent who says 'You will be the death of me' or 'I'll go away and leave you' threatens a child's security, and it has added potency if there is any aspect of real life to give the threat credence.

Another characteristic of this age group is a preoccupation with being 'good or bad' and 'powerful or little'. Ideally, a child should have the chance to experience all of these states and play is a good vehicle for achieving this. It relieves some of the anxieties that are common at this age. Children often suffer from nightmares (their imagination is not sufficiently developed for these to occur earlier) and they are frequently afraid of the dark or going upstairs. Bedtimes can become particularly fraught and parental reassurance is necessary, plus practical measures such as a nightlight. Parents should, of course, neither ridicule a child for believing there is a bad giant at the top of the stairs nor support the fantasy by pretending to talk to it!

The primary school years

The years between the start of school and the beginning of adolescence tend to be the time recalled with nostalgia by adults and the most rewarding for parents. Children are past the stage of minute-by-minute dependence and there are none of the conflicts associated with parenting teenagers. Parents see their children growing in competence and confidence and it sometimes offers them a second chance to experience childhood pleasures. Those who cheer on the touchline at school football matches are an example.

Entry into school means that a child has to manage in a large group and mix with children who have been brought up with different rules. Children are asked questions about themselves in class and, not surprisingly, this is the time when they come home and ask more about their family circumstances. However, younger children are normally satisfied with truthful factual answers and are less concerned and interested in the feelings associated with relationships than are older children. Whilst activities and friendships outside the family become very important during these years, children continue to conform and to identify with the values and attitudes of their own family. This can of course pose a dilemma for a child in substitute care who has to juggle with competing standards. Although the outside world beckons, the family retains its importance as a 'secure base' and a refuge when playground life and the demands of the classroom tax the child's ability to cope.

The psychological task for the primary school years is to acquire what Erikson called 'a sense of industry'. In fact children of this age are keen to work and, while it may not always be on classroom tasks, a glance at any playground will reveal children engaged in all manner of activities. Opportunities to acquire skills are important at this age and children want their achievements recorded in a tangible form; badges and certificates are eagerly sought. Friendships, particularly in groups, are part of the schoolchild's development. A child learns that s/he has to give up some of her or his own wishes in exchange for group membership. The group, however, offers excitement that is entirely secret from the adult world, and by the time children are 9 or 10 years old the group will have elaborate rules and maybe a den *and* a secret password.

Finally, it is important to take into account how children in this age group view fairness in their dealings with others. Being fair is a highly-rated quality and generally it means 'treating everyone the same'. Children are very resistant to the notion that anyone should receive preferential treatment on the basis of need. Their thinking is termed as 'concrete', as opposed to the teenager's capacity to deal in abstract concepts. If, for example, an adult wishes to challenge a child about having won a game by cheating, the discussion is more fruitful if it takes place in relation to a specific example: 'Would you think someone had really won the game if you knew s/he had cheated?'

Into adolescence

This period of life covers the change from being a dependent child to becoming a young adult. The change is physical as well as emotional and the adolescent thinks and acts differently from the childhood years. The notion that adolescence is inescapably 'difficult' is challenged by those who maintain that most adolescents get on well with their parents, feel supported by them and enjoy confiding relationships. Nevertheless, others maintain that the changes inherent in becoming an adolescent mean a degree of tension is unavoidable.

Anna Freud (1965) described the adolescent in the following terms:

> Adolescents are excessively egotistical, regarding themselves as the centre of the universe and the sole object of interest, and yet at no time in later life are they capable of so much self-sacrifice and devotion. They form the most passionate love relationships only to break them . . . . on the one hand they throw themselves into the life of the community, on the other have an overpowering longing for solitude . . . . they are selfish and materially minded and at the same time full of lofty idealism.

This list of contradictions would find favour with a parent who was puzzled when her son lectured her about animal rights, having forgotten to feed the dog when the rest of the family was away!

The relationship between an adolescent and her or his parents changes from the relative intimacy and involvement of the school years to a detachment from family life. Instead s/he invests in relationships with other young people. This does not mean that the parenting task is complete. Winnicott maintains that the adolescent 'needs to defy in a setting in which dependence is met and can be relied on to be met'. Whilst this makes sound emotional sense, it also makes for a period of life when both parents and children regard each other as 'unreasonable'. The adolescent rarely wants to wait for anything, while the parent anticipates hazards and the child's ability to cope; hence, 'Don't you trust me?' becomes a familiar refrain.

Adolescent relationships are often short-lived because they are based on a particular need of the moment; it may be a liking for the same music or someone who is 'a good laugh'. When such friendships founder, the adolescent feels acutely lonely. Such exploration should be seen in positive terms. An adolescent is seeking to establish what s/he is and will become. While the process may exasperate adults, the end product is a well-rooted and resilient adult. The adolescent who follows parental prescription or is too fearful to experiment is more vulnerable in adult life.

Conclusion

The journey from dependence to self-reliance can be accomplished more easily if the child has an 'average expectable environment'. Children who need the help of social workers have by definition experienced adversity and therefore their development is in danger of being derailed. We have seen that until a child reaches adolescence the primary need is for care. Usually, children will say that they want to remain with whoever is providing that security and will, if encouraged to do so, reject a parent. But by the time a child reaches the teenage years the lure of independence and establishing adult status takes over from a need to be parented. Rarely will adolescents trade-in freedom for security, particularly if they have little experience of caring adults.

Children manage difficult changes more easily if they are able to anticipate and prepare for them. They feel less 'done to' and more in control of events. If preparation is impossible, then the child has to absorb the change retrospectively. Whichever way it happens, the child depends on adults to take time to explain and understand her or his responses, whether expressed in behaviour or in words.

References

Bowlby, J. (1979) *The Making and Breaking of Affectional Bonds*. London: Tavistock.

Erikson, E. H. (1959) *Identity and the Life Cycle*. New York, NY.: International Universities Press.

Fahlberg, V. (1994) *A Child's Journey Through Placement* (UK edition). London: British Agencies for Adoption and Fostering.

Freud, A. (1965) *Normality and Pathology in Childhood: Assessments of Development*. New York, NY.: International Universities Press.

Klein, M. (1986) in Mitchell, J. (ed.) *The Selected Melanie Klein*. London: Penguin.

Winnicott, D. (1971) *Playing and Reality*. London: Penguin.

CHAPTER 11

COMMUNICATING WITH CHILDREN AND ASCERTAINING THEIR WISHES AND FEELINGS
Marian Brandon

There is a laudable sentiment in *The Challenge of Partnership in Child Protection* (Department of Health 1995): 'Establishing a child's wishes and feelings is a first step towards enabling their participation.' Laudable, yes, but not without its problems.

Workers need particular skills and knowledge to make the shift to listening to what children say themselves, rather than just hearing what others are saying about them. Communicating effectively with children must be the first step towards ascertaining their wishes and feelings but this can only be attempted after a relationship has been developed. Gauging a child's evolving capacity to know and articulate her or his views comes as a part of the work with the child and must be set in the context of that person's individual circumstances. The child will have hopes, aspirations and anxieties about many matters, not just the particular decision at issue. Professional preoccupations may not coincide with the child's own concerns.

The requirement to ascertain children's wishes and feelings first appeared in the 1980 Children Act. Since then, children in 'care' have had some rights to have their views taken into consideration when decisions are being made that affect them. With the later Children Act 1989 it could be argued that the emphasis on 'non-intervention' underlines the responsibilities of families and parents to determine what is best for children, implicitly denying the child an autonomous voice. Yet the 1989 Act contains within it competing value positions, including an acceptance that children have rights as individuals rather than the rights that their parents or carers hold 'in trust' for them. In this more recent legislation, children are given a voice by the reappearance of a more extensive need to consult children and find out their views. These various sections of the Act apply to all children coming into the orbit of the courts in consideration of any order and in contested divorce cases. In social services' family support work, it applies to children in accommodation or on the threshold of accommodation (Section 22) where the child's wishes and feelings are ascertained alongside those of others 'as far as is practicable'. In child protection work it has effect from the point of the initial investigation (Department of Health 1991 and 1995).

In any matter that comes before the court, the welfare of the child is also considered individually and determined by reference to a checklist (Section 1.3) that has at its core the 'ascertainable wishes and feelings of the child (considered in the light of his age and understanding)'. The court is not constrained to act on these wishes and case law has determined that the court should indeed disregard them if the child's welfare so demands. The court is obliged, however, to do more than pay lip-service to the child's views. Although the 'welfare checklist' is intended for matters brought before the courts, it is used widely by workers to help them to consider children as individuals within their own family and cultural context, having individual needs and their own views.

All children are entitled to a degree of choice and influence over their own daily lives but not all children want to be held responsible for major decisions that present them with divided loyalties. The Children Act 1989, in Volume 3 of the Guidance, claims that children should not be overburdened with decision-making. Yet Volume 6 of the Guidance, concerned with children with disabilities, suggests that the 'burden' may come because of a lack of support to help children learn to make decisions and appropriate judgements: 'Learning to make well informed choices should be part of every child's experiences.' (Guidance Vol. 6 1991 p.14)

The 1989 United Nations Convention on the Rights of the Child asserts the child's right to a voice but also acknowledges limitations to the extent to which the child's views should be acted upon. For example, Article 12 states:

> The child who is capable of forming his or her own views [has] the right to express
> those views freely in all matters affecting the child, the views of the child being
> given due weight in accordance with the age and understanding.

At the heart of this is the debate concerning the way in which age and maturity are determined and interpreted, and the extent to which any child can be considered to know what is in her or his best interests.

It is ironic that the children in the most turmoil and distress are the ones who are most often asked their wishes and feelings. There is no parallel requirement in daily life for parents or schools to listen to the views of children and give them due consideration. On the whole, children lack practice in exercising choices about their daily lives, over small issues as well as larger ones. A student social worker commented thus about an 8-year-old boy she was working with:

> Adam was often bemused at being asked his views or feelings as his experience had
> been one of having no say over events in the family. He was very confused and
> unable to express his views consistently.

Similarly, a child on an Interim Care Order as a result of a child protection investigation can find that three, four or more professionals are 'ascertaining the child's wishes and feelings'. It may be possible for none of these professionals to be acting on what the child has said. Lynes and Goddard (1995) quote a 14-year-old boy's experience of reviews: 'They listen to you but they don't do anything, or it seems like that anyway.'

How can we make the exercise of ascertaining wishes and feelings meaningful for the child and not a frustrating and bewildering intrusion? This is the focus of the remainder of this chapter.

Basic principles for communicating with children

Here are three key principles:

1. Understand the context of your practice as a social worker with children in general. A good starting point is *The Care of Children: Principles and Practice in Regulations and Guidance* (DoH 1989), which summarises this context. Be especially aware of the family setting.
2. Establish a relationship and develop the resources and skills necessary to be attentive to the child. With this comes the willingness to respect the child and to see things from the child's point of view, be it through conversation, play or observation of the child's behaviour. Understand the child in her or his particular context. What does 'expressing a view' mean to this individual child, in the context of her or his family and circumstances? Develop a good understanding of child development so that expectations are appropriate to the stage of development and level of understanding. How will you tailor your work with children to their developmental level?
3. Understand the child's own characteristics. Develop practical and personal resources to enable the work to be done. This includes creating the time and space to develop a relationship to establish the child's view of the world.

Family setting

The long-term aims of work to ascertain the child's wishes and feelings should be for that child to develop the capacity to exercise choice and have informed views as a maturing young person and as an adult citizen. The child needs to practise these skills within the family, and work undertaken should reinforce rather than undermine this possibility. If the child is not with the birth family but in a foster home or residential setting, then there are two 'families' to be borne in mind and the child's links with their origins should be remembered.

Parents and carers need information and support to reassure them that their parental role with the child is not being undermined. The family may have strong views about whether their child should be offered a say, and this may be linked to particular religious or cultural attitudes about the role and place of children. If a family thinks that the child's views should not be represented separately from the parents, what difference will it make to the child's relationship with the family if the social worker transgresses these beliefs? If English is the family's second language, then ensuring understanding on all sides becomes more crucial and it is important to consider using an interpreter. If so, assurances should be made that the interpreter is acceptable to the family and child.

Developing resources

Techniques and resources should be adapted for each individual child, but it is useful to start with some basic play materials.

Again, the materials used should be those with which you feel comfortable. You need to practise using them in advance. Most workers feel at ease using pens and paper but even this basic material can include paper of different colours, so the child has a choice, and other simple props like stars or stickers. Creating a star picture, with the child at the centre of the constellation of family, friends and important people in the child's life, is a simple way of helping the child to talk about life at home or school or in other settings. Adolescents may be wary of gimmicks such as stars, but some like them and appreciate being offered a choice about using them. Others may be content just to talk, or to write or draw with you.

It is not essential to have dedicated space to work with children. If your materials are selected carefully, they can be portable and a lot of work can be done in the child's own home. Negotiations can also be undertaken with the child and her or his parents or carers about whether it would be better to use the child's own room, or whether arrangements can be made to use the kitchen or a downstairs area that can be kept private for the period of time you will need. You will not be able to create the intensity of play therapy but it will be easier to link the work with the child back in with the family. For longer-term work the pattern can be varied so that trips out can be made with the child.

What can be expected of children at different ages and stages and their 'evolving maturity' will obviously be affected by their individual experiences. The overall maturity of a 10-year-old who has lived through several years of sexual abuse will be different from a similar child without this background. Many children who come to the attention of social services because they are in need, or are suffering significant harm, may take on responsibilities for their own care or those of siblings and appear precociously mature. Their 'true' cognitive and emotional maturity may not match their apparent coping abilities. It is important to pitch the work at the right level so that the child will understand what is being asked and benefit from her or his time with you.

The child's own characteristics

When planning the work it is essential to seek out background details to make sense of the child, as well as the family background and current circumstances. Hasty appearances to ask children what they want followed by the disappearance of the questioner will do more harm than good.

The child needs to be understood as an individual in her or his own right. Their age, sex, developmental stage and experiences to date need to be considered at the planning stage and throughout the involvement. There is a need to discover the child's particular abilities, or disabilities and losses, as well as previous experiences of professional helpers.

Assurances are needed about how much information will be fed back to parents or carers. Children are increasingly aware of the impact of telling professionals their worries, and fear that things may be made worse, not better.

Calls to the 'ChildLine' telephone number for children in care have demonstrated how lacking in trust, isolated and troubled many children feel when away from their birth families, either in residential or foster care. It would appear that professionals' attempts to communicate are not always successful. In many ways ChildLine can act as a rehearsal for children expressing their views to carers or social workers, but in an ideal situation the child should feel able to talk about her or his concerns to people close at hand.

The following practice guide is a starting point only, but can be helpful in tailoring the work to the individual child.

The pre-school child

Listening to very young children requires heightened observational skills. The fine detail of how they behave and how they exhibit pleasure and curiosity, anger, stress or anxiety needs to be studied. Ascertaining wishes and feelings for this age group will require examining the way in which children relate to important people around them. Attachment theory can make sense of these observations and provides helpful explanations for behaviour and relationships.

Play offers the perfect medium through which a child's concerns and preoccupations can be observed and through which you can develop a relationship. Interpreting play needs considerable care. Parents, nursery workers or others may be well placed to help the social worker to put the play in its context. Pugh and Rouse Selleck (1996) explain that many young children cope with stress through play:

> Rich fantasy play needs to be taken seriously instead of dismissing weapons and noisy activities as bad behaviour or problems . . . . Observations of patterns in play can help parents and professionals to listen to children thinking and learning.

5- to 11-year-olds

As children reach school age they begin to make the shift towards more highly developed mental processes and become better able to focus their attention. But the 5- or 6-year-old child who is fluent in language and can tell a good joke still has difficulty in seeing things from different perspectives. Things tend to be all good or all bad; friends are loved or hated. Susan Harter's work on children's self-esteem has shown that sometime between the age of 5 and 7 a child is likely to start making judgements that are more differentiated. When this happens, children can see themselves as, for example, good at some things but not others. Not until the age of 8, however, do children depict themselves or others as 'part smart and part dumb' (Harter 1983) and can conceive of this beyond the domain of school to realise that they can make smart (wise or sensible) decisions at home too.

In terms of working with the child, mixing play with some simple questions becomes possible. But Garbarino and Stott (1992) provide a note of caution:

> The basic approach is to take nothing for granted, to rely on modes of communication familiar to the child, and to constantly be on the alert to the possibility of misunderstanding in both directions.

Young school children also are very sensitive to what they perceive as adult expectations and are likely to tell a social worker what they think she or he wants to hear.

Concrete thinking is a powerful force for all children in the 5-to-11 age range. Ask a child who they are 'close to' in the family and up to the age of 11 or so you risk the child telling you about the person sitting nearest to them. Use of language needs to be given careful thought and kept simple.

12-year-olds and above

From 12 or so onwards, children are moving away from concrete thinking to acquire more sophisticated cognitive skills. For some children this is not achieved until 15 or later, and for some others not at all. Young people who are at this level should be able to think about the possible as well as the actual and can think and make choices about the future. Determining decisions for children who have reached this stage is developmentally possible, but emotional maturity may not coincide with cognitive ability.

The degree to which a young person should be responsible for major decisions will depend very much on individual circumstances. Many older children, particularly in divorce circumstances, do not want to be held responsible for letting down a parent by making a choice in favour of one rather than the other.

In most cases older children will want to exercise their opinions, even if the outcome is not perfect. For example, a 14-year-old Bosnian Muslim boy, Stefan, was cognitively and emotionally mature but confused by the competing cultural demands of his family and the Western culture at school, which offered more say to children. He voiced his view at the child protection conference that his father should not have beaten him when he went against his parents' wishes. The family were outraged that outside professionals were brought in to regulate their family life, and felt that they knew best how to protect and promote Stefan's interests. Stefan had mixed feelings about the outcome of these events because he had lost his family's trust. He was clear, however, that his father did not have the right to beat him in any circumstances and that his views in this must be respected.

Conclusion

For all ages of children there are two constant themes that need to be borne in mind if working with them to ascertain their wishes and feelings is also to help them to exercise choice and control over their lives as they mature. These two themes are: choice and consent; and making sure the child's views can be acted on.

Choice and consent

There is a responsibility on all workers to ensure that the child has a degree of control and choice in the work done and consents actively to answering questions, playing games, or choosing where the 'play-work' is to take place. Until children are 10 or 11 they may not be able to say they don't know, can't remember or don't fully understand. It is the worker's responsibility to monitor and assess the child's ability and receptivity to the work being done. Be alert to the child's interest and enthusiasm; watch the child's body language for signs of stress. Intersperse drawing with talking. Let the child choose a new activity.

Making sure the child's views can be acted on

Avoid being too fixed about what you think is of major concern to the child. Understand children's concerns from their whole context: their life at school, or with grandparents, as well as at home; problems with friends as well as with relatives. Try to establish whether her or his views change from day to day, or whether you are being told merely what the child wants you to hear.

Because the child may not be allowed or may not want the final say in major decisions, it is essential that some aspects of the child's views be acted on. Tackling some worries, like bullying at school, may make living with largely irresolvable family problems easier to cope with. Helping even very young children to have a say in day-to-day matters, so that they see their opinions are important, can improve the quality of their lives.

Children interviewed in the study 'Safeguarding Children with the Children Act 1989' told us they wanted to see their social worker often enough so that the latter could get to know the child as a person. They also wanted social workers to 'confirm decisions' with children. Finally they said that they could tell whether or not a worker was really listening: 'Sometimes they listen; sometimes they just keep chattering to your mum.'

References:

Department of Health (1995) *The Challenge of Partnership in Child Protection: Practice Guide.* London: HMSO.

Department of Health with the Home Office, Department of Education and Science and the Welsh Office (1991) *Working Together Under the Children Act 1989: A guide to arrangements for inter-agency co-operation for the protection of children from abuse.* London: HMSO.

Garbarino, J. and Stott, F. M. (1992) *What Children Can Tell Us: Eliciting, Interpreting, and Evaluating Critical Information from Children.* San Francisco, Calif.: Jossey-Bass, p. 179.

Harter, S. (1983) 'A Developmental Perspective on the Self-System' in Mussen, P. H. (ed.) *Handbook of Child Psychology,* 4th edition. Basingstoke: John Wiley & Sons.

Lynes, D. and Goddard, J. (1995) *The View from the Front: The User View of Child Care in Norfolk.* Norwich: Norfolk County Council Social Services.

Pugh, G. and Rouse Selleck, D. (1996) 'Listening to and communicating with young children' in Davie, R., Upton, G. and Varna, V. (eds) *The Voice of the Child: a handbook for professionals,* Brighton: Falmer Press, p. 11.

CHAPTER 12

CHILDREN WITH COMMUNICATION DIFFICULTIES
Janet Lees

Every child communicates. That communication may be vocal, like crying; gestural, like pointing or sign language; affective, like hugging; motoric, like pushing or pulling; verbal, like speech; electronic, as with a communication device like 'Liberator' or 'Touch Talker'; pictorial, with photos, pictures or symbols; written, with letters and words; or bodily, by just being there. In fact there are many different ways of classifying modes or methods of communication. Most children use several in their total communication style.

All that is required for effective communication is one person to send a 'message' and one person to receive it. A message may be both sent and received in many different ways. The method of conveying and decoding the message may also affect its interpretation. Within this broad definition of communication, it might seem that the term 'children with communication difficulties' has no place. If every child communicates, it might seem to be just a matter of letting it all happen through any modality. However, our society is biased towards verbal communication. It considers speech to be the pinnacle of human achievement as far as communication is concerned and it therefore places more value on verbal communication than on any other mode. This often means that it also places more value on verbal communicators than on those whose modes of communication are non-verbal. In this respect medical science, and speech and language therapy, use the term 'children with communication disorders' for those children who communicate predominately through a mode or modes not used by the verbal majority of their peer group.

The development of communication skills

The majority of children learn to communicate adequately using verbal language by the age of 5 and that development proceeds in a common time-frame and order. When a child's communication development usually falls outside of this generally recognised pattern, this may cause concern to the child's family, school teachers, medical practitioners and other health care workers – and to the children themselves. Two main alternative patterns of development are described: delayed development and deviant, or disordered, development. Children with delayed development are thought usually to be progressing at a slower rate than their peers, whilst those with deviant, or disordered, development are usually described as developing skills in a different pattern or order from their peers. The implication is that children with delayed communication development might be able to catch up with their peers, whilst those with a more deviant pattern, although they are likely to make progress, will continue to communicate in ways not always characteristic of their peer group. Between 3 per cent and 8 per cent of the pre-school population have significant difficulties in the development of speech and language.

Children with communication disorders

Children with delayed or disordered development in communication skills can still: communicate, although perhaps with a reduced range of skills; be educated, although they may have special educational needs; function socially, although their range of social contacts may be reduced; make progress, as all children continue to develop, however slowly.

Children with communication disorders might have difficulty:

- moving or co-ordinating the organs of speech production (motor speech disorders);
- receiving the sound of speech (hearing impairments);
- processing the sounds of speech (central auditory processing difficulties);
- processing the language they hear (receptive language disorders);
- accessing the language they have;
- with language or speech (expressive language disorders);
- matching the appropriate form of communication to the social situation (disorders of language use, pragmatic disorders, autistic spectrum disorders, etc.);
- with written language (dyslexias and dysgraphias);
- with attending to communication (attention deficit disorders);
- in the fluency of their speech (stammering);
- by choosing to communicate only in certain situations (selective mutism).

These difficulties may occur simultaneously. They may be present from the beginning of a child's communication development or be acquired during childhood in the general population. The former reason is probably at least ten times as common as the latter.

Experience of communication from the child's perspective

Although there are few studies of the experience of communication difficulty from the child's perspective, there have been a few examples more recently in which people with a wide range of communication difficulties have 'spoken for themselves'. They often comment on the 'Does He Take Sugar?' Syndrome that appears to affect a large proportion of the general population. Features of this behaviour include: assuming that all people with communication difficulties are unable to express themselves in any way; failing to listen to such people; failing to take sufficient time to interact with them; and regarding them as less than human. For example, Reid and Button (1995) record the experiences of Anna, a 13-year-old girl diagnosed as language-impaired at the age of 5. She says 'I usually feel mad.' And: 'Sometimes I feel frustrated because I'm in there.'

She describes her experiences of integration in a mainstream context:

> I couldn't even sit at their desks with them. I always had to be by myself at a different table. And I was pretty sad. They helped me but they didn't really *want* to help me.

Anna concludes:

> So I get along with it sometimes. And it's pretty hard.

All children begin communicating within the first hours of life. These basic communications are gradually built upon through the major part of the first year of life. For children with significant difficulties in early communicative interaction, in most cases these are demonstrable by the end of the first year of life. What is not yet clear is whether such children really do develop their communication skills so very differently in this early period; whether factors concerning the carer, like depression or expectation, affect the development of these skills; or whether factors intrinsic to both child and carer contribute to the difference in communication development at this stage.

In their reports of communication impairment in childhood, professionals note the following:

1. Communication development in children extends well beyond the fifth year, such that there are important stages in the development of more advanced communication skills – including vocabulary, syntax and pragmatic meaning – well into the teenage years.
2. Early brain injury (under 5 years of age) is not an irreversible phenomenon but it can certainly limit communication and other cognitive potential, particularly the acquisition of written language skills.
3. The needs of severely communication-impaired children are properly the concern of a child-centred multidisciplinary team. The team includes the child's family or carers and draws skills from education, social and medical well as from voluntary services.
4. Extreme deprivation and abuse affects the communication development of children and their recovery.

It has been suggested that the inability of disabled children to communicate experiences is one of the factors that make them, as a group, more vulnerable to abuse. Also, the assumption that communication-impaired children are 'less human' because of their communication difficulty has played a role in their abuse. The contention is that the abuse of someone who is 'less than human' is therefore 'not that inhumane' and is based on the observation that communication-impaired children, as children with disabilities, are repeatedly stigmatised in our society, amounting to a 'licence to abuse'. In this way, society's response to disability may be a factor in the perpetration of abuse on children with disabilities, including communication impairments.

The improvement of communication channels for children with disabilities is important so that disclosure of the abuse is made easier. It is noted that children with communication difficulties may initiate conversations less than their peers and may only respond in reply to direct questions. For those for whom imitation and repetition of a model is an important part of providing a verbal response, disclosure is even more difficult to facilitate. Specific difficulties in comprehending may occur for children with learning difficulties, such that they may not understand that they are being abused.

Communication disorder and child protection enquiries

How might a child with a communication disorder take part in child protection enquiries? Clearly, this will depend both on the child and the situation. Therefore, only general points can be made here in respect of the particular needs of children with different types of communication difficulties.

Motor speech disorders

Children with motor speech problems may have general motor problems, such as cerebral palsy, or specific difficulties with speech production, such as dyspraxia.

For those children with general motor problems considerations about mobility may also need attention. Where motor speech problems are severe, the child may be unable to articulate or vocalise at all. In such situations augmentative and alternative communication strategies are important. Their selection will depend on the general motor competence and cognitive ability of the child. They may include the use of 'low-tech' systems such as signs and symbol systems, alphabet and photograph boards or books, to 'high-tech' systems including electronic communicators such as 'Liberator'. Where children use these methods of communication, a facilitator or translator may be required. Furthermore, it will be important to remember that some children will use telegrammatic language, in which case communication may take longer than its verbal equivalent.

Hearing impairment

Children with hearing impairments may have temporary or permanent hearing loss. Temporary fluctuating hearing loss due to otitis media is a common condition of childhood. Such problems may make children inattentive or impair their comprehension of spoken language. This kind of hearing problem usually is readily treated with antibiotics or myringotimies and grommets and then should resolve fairly quickly. Children with permanent hearing impairments may be sign-language users or hearing-aid users or both; they may also lip-read.

Involving a child with hearing impairment in child protection may mean: ensuring that a hearing aid and loop system are functioning appropriately; ensuring the availability of sign-language users for interpretation if necessary; giving consideration to the acoustic properties and lighting used to facilitate lip-reading; ensuring the availability of a person used to the child's speech if it is unintelligible; taking time to ensure the child has understood what has been said; and, if appropriate, making information available in a written form to back up comprehension.

Language difficulties

Children with delayed or disordered language may have problems both in understanding what is said to them or expressing themselves in generally accepted linguistic forms (or both). They may augment their communication with sign and symbol systems. Expressive language may be marked by errors of form (grammar or speech-sound system), content (vocabulary limitations, word-finding difficulties) or use (pragmatics). The more advanced aspects of language development, such as narrative or the use of complex sentences, is more likely to be impaired. Thus children may use telegrammatic language, or only use the present tense, or have difficulty with pronouns such that they use 'he' for 'she' or vice versa. Such children will need someone familiar with their communication difficulty to act as a facilitator or translator – such a person may know what kind of cues the child uses to aid word-finding. It is important to note that some language-impaired children who were abused in the pre-verbal stage of their development later have been able to report these experiences despite lacking sufficient language to report the abuse when it occurred (Hewitt 1994).

Speech difficulties

This broad category refers to children whose speech is difficult to understand because of delay or deviancy in the development of the speech-sound system. For some children, structural factors contribute to this (for example, a child with a cleft palate). For others, hearing loss may be a contributory factor. But for the majority it is just a case of slower maturity of that aspect of the language system. When children are unintelligible for several years, especially beyond the age of 5, then augmentative or alternative systems that include signing and symbols may be used to clarify ambiguity; therefore, such children may need the assistance of a translator or facilitator to ensure that they are understood.

Stammering

Children and young people may have difficulty with speech fluency such that their speech is characterised by a significant proportion of hesitations and repetition. Other characteristics include the prolongation of some sounds, as well as a complete inability to produce sounds at all – called 'blocking' – all of which may be accompanied by facial grimaces or habitual body postures and poorly developed social communication skills. Language development also may be delayed or deviant. In the early stages (that is, under 7 years) stammering rarely is very severe and may disappear completely for some periods. This is also the time when a child is most likely to 'grow out of it' and probably reflects changes in developmental maturity, the acquisition of new communication skills or changes in the child's environment. If stammering persists, particularly beyond the first part of childhood and into adolescence, it may be accompanied by social interaction and integration difficulties, including bullying at school.

Children may be taught to use a range of techniques to increase their control of speech fluency, including relaxation and posture control, social communication skills, and specific techniques such as the slowing and prolonging of speech. Such work can be done individually or in small groups and can include role-play. On the whole, most children who stammer are fluent some of the time, can find a technique or combination of techniques that helps increase fluency and can experience increased disfluency in situations when pressure to use fluent speech is increased – for example, on the telephone or in situations of increased stress.

Involving in child protection a child who stammers will require: an understanding of the severity of the difficulty and how this is affected by different situations and circumstances; an understanding of the techniques the child employs to increase fluency, including relaxation, postural considerations, social communication skills and specific speech techniques such as 'prolonged speech'; and a consideration of the possible opportunities for the child to role-play similar situations in advance. For the very disfluent child, sufficient time and appropriate responses to reassure her or him that s/he can stammer as freely as necessary will be important and helpful.

Autistic spectrum disorders

Children with autism and related disorders have difficulty in their development of cognitive, social and communicative abilities. There is no one 'typical' pattern but rather a spectrum of developmental difficulties is seen, ranging from children with good cognitive skills and mild social and communication impairments, to more seriously affected individuals in all three domains. Communication difficulties combine to include speech and language disorders as well as social communication disorders, so that most autistic children are more communication-impaired than their speech- and language-impaired peers.

The intent to use communication socially is a crucial part of communication development and is a key deficit in autism. These children often have a limited range of social contacts, may not communicate at all with strangers, or may show little or no awareness of the usual social constraints on communication. Also the development of their play is usually impaired and may involve long rituals, obsessive components and reduced creativity.

Facilitated communication is used with some autistic children. This term refers to a range of methods by which the child is 'guided' to type or spell out their communicative attempts. The approach has had a number of critics, who point out that it is all too easy for the facilitator to 'choose' what the child communicates. However, it is clear that, increasingly, as a method by which socially impaired children might communicate important life events (including abuse), it cannot be ignored and needs to be evaluated properly. Amongst the criteria suggested are that typographical errors, phonetic spelling, phrases and idioms are likely to be specific to the individual child. Also, the content will not be known to the facilitator – something that can be verified. Obviously the ideas and concepts expressed should be appropriate to the child's social and educational background, compared with the level of skills demonstrated in other areas. However, it is clear that authors of these studies recognise that this work may not yet be up to a standard usable in criminal or juvenile legal proceedings (Heckler 1994; Howlin and Jones 1996).

Dyslexia

Dyslexia is a disorder of written language but may occur with other speech and language difficulties. It may occur as a developmental difficulty or following acquired brain injury. Involving a child or young person with dyslexia in child protection issues means being aware of the amount of reading and writing that is assumed as part of the process. Equally, as dyslexia may be only the 'tip of the iceberg', or the most obvious part of the child's communication difficulty, it is important not to overload the child's capacity to process different types of information simultaneously.

Selective mutism

A child with selective mutism also may have significant speech and language delay or disorder. However, the main consideration will be in what situations and with whom the child is willing and able to communicate. It is not unusual for children who survive abuse to adopt a strategy of selective mutism.

Children may have more than one of the above communication difficulties at the same time. Comprehensive assessment by a speech and language therapist will be required to provide a detailed profile of a child's communicative abilities.

Summary of needs

Children with communication difficulties:

1. are likely to need more time to communicate;
2. may have even greater difficulty under stress;
3. may need to use specific equipment, from a loop system, radio microphone or an electronic communication aid;
4. may need specific people to help them communicate more effectively, including a translator or a facilitator who, if used, must be properly trained;
5. may choose not to communicate in some situations or in the presence of some people.

Conclusion

Some people who have come through difficult periods of their lives can, later on, explain the early difficulties they had expressing themselves during such periods. 'I could never tell anyone' is a common theme of these later reflections. For the child with communication disorders 'I could never tell anyone' may be compounded by a whole range of physical and mental factors and by the lack of awareness of these factors by other workers. Again, we need to remember that every child communicates; it is a skilled task to ensure that they can communicate about their life experiences as fully as possible.

References

Heckler, S. (1994) 'Facilitated Communication: A response to child protection', *Child Abuse and Neglect,* 18, pp. 495–503.

Hewitt, S. K. (1994) 'Pre-verbal Sexual Abuse: What two children report in later years', *Child Abuse and Neglect,* 18, pp. 821–26.

Howlin, P. and Jones, D. P. H. (1996) 'An assessment approach to abuse allegations made through facilitated communication', *Child Abuse and Neglect,* 20, pp. 103–10.

Reid, D. K. and Button, L. J. (1995) 'Anna's story: narratives of personal experience about being labelled learning disabled', *Journal of Learning Disabilities*, 28(10), pp. 602–14.

CHAPTER 13

THE IMPORTANCE OF RELATIONSHIPS
David Shemmings

Whenever we think about working with people, especially young people, we know intuitively that to be successful it is essential to gain their trust and confidence. But are we sure what we are supposed to do exactly; we know that we *have* to, but are we sure *how* to?

In the United States in the mid-1960s a massive programme of research began, the central aim of which was to fathom out why some 'helpers' ('counsellors', 'therapists', 'psychotherapists', etc.) seemed to be more effective than others. Was it the particular form of intervention they used, or was it their skill in matching their intervention to the specific problems of the other person? Was it connected to the way in which the two parties got on together; was it more a matter of chemistry than skill? Was it just luck? And what is meant by 'effective' anyway? There followed an unprecedented number of studies, conducted mainly by Robert Carkhuff alongside numerous colleagues and associates – for example with B. G. Berenson (Carkhuff and Berenson 1967).

Each time the statistical tests were completed, the same conclusions were found: the variable that accounted for more differences in successful helping encounters than any other was the helper's ability to bring to the relationship certain qualities and skills. It was not what helpers had in their 'tool-kit' that mattered; it was what they as people brought to the relationship that determined whether what followed would work. Social workers and other members of the helping professions have claimed this to be true ever since. But what is meant exactly when a professional says 'I shall have to develop a good relationship with this child before she will trust me with some of her pain.'?

As Carl Rogers (1951) had argued earlier, as both a clinician and a theorist, similarly the American studies of the 1960s concluded that three qualities in the helper were essential for trust to develop: *respect, genuineness* and *warmth*. In addition, the helper would have to bring three skills to the early stages of the relationship: *attending, listening* and *empathy*. The central difference between Rogers and Carkhuff was the extent to which they saw these qualities and skills as *necessary* or *sufficient*. Rogers believed that they were necessary and sufficient, whereas Carkhuff saw them as necessary but not sufficient. Rogers was convinced that if helpers could create the 'core conditions of a therapeutic relationship' by bringing these skills and qualities to it then, of itself, this would be enough to energise the creative potential of most people into any subsequent action needed to alleviate 'personal' problems. Of course, Rogers was not saying that 'understanding' would pay the rent of a low-income family or that 'compassion' would stop racist attacks or bullying. He always restricted himself to what would help others talk about their 'inner' conflicts and tensions.

Carkhuff saw the nature of these core conditions differently. Of course helpers should possess them in abundance, but they were not enough in themselves to provide the assurance that anything would happen afterwards to dissolve problems. For him they were the foundations for what follows; for Rogers they comprised the whole structure. In the mid-1970s Gerard Egan took the research further, in particular into the field of training. With the publication of *The Skilled Helper* in 1975 he began his lifelong project into the different stages, qualities and skills needed during helping processes. Egan's work stands out as the most thorough study into the ways people decide to trust others, talk about the things that are causing them discomfort in their lives, and then find the inner resources to do something about them. In this chapter, I quote widely from *The Skilled Helper,* which is now in its fifth edition (Egan 1994).

Some things have moved on since the early research, which the following extract from *The Skilled Helper* illustrates:

> The idea of one perfect kind of helping relationship is a myth. Different clients have different needs, and these needs are best met through different kinds of relationships. One client may work best with a helper who expresses a great deal of warmth; another might work best with a helper who is more objective and businesslike. Some clients come to counselling with a fear of intimacy: they may be put off by helpers who, right from the beginning, communicate a great deal of empathy and warmth. Effective helpers use a mix of skills and techniques tailored to the kind of relationship that is right for each client.

But most of the other findings have stood the test of time. In particular, three apply to the involvement of children:

> firstly, that to help someone we have to show them that we are prepared to listen to where 'they are', and not keep telling them where 'we are'; secondly, and somewhat obviously, we cannot do this very easily if the person does not want to communicate with us; and, thirdly, they will only communicate with us if they think we will listen and then help them to do something about what is bothering them.

It is not difficult to apply these findings to the involvement of children and young people in family support and child protection processes, but there are two key differences. First, such children have not always asked for, or knew they needed, our help; it may have been imposed on them – indeed, they may be extremely unwilling and unco-operative. Secondly, professionals often have to find out the 'wishes and feelings' of a young person by a fixed deadline – for example, by a date set for a statutory review or for a court hearing. Imagine, after a frightening incident, someone coming to you and saying:

> I know we've never met but could you just tell me what your wishes and feelings are about . . . . Oh, by the way, what you say will be extremely important in determining where you live, who you live with, and a whole lot of other things concerning your future. (Egan 1994)

These differences mean that professionals in the field of family support and child protection have to be above-average at gaining the trust and confidence of young people, and they need to be able to do it to order; not for them the luxury of willing clients and leather upholstery.

In addition, these professionals must demonstrate by their actions that they are trustworthy. They can never ask a young person to 'trust me'; they have to prove themselves by offering *demonstrable trust* (Shemmings and Shemmings 1996). The metaphor of 'trust-as-faith' has to be changed to one of 'trust-as-proof'. The trouble is that, if we pay regard to Ian Butler's and Howard Williamson's findings to date (outlined earlier in Chapter 2), professionals do not get a very good press from young people when it comes to listening.

What can be learned from the research on 'relationship skills' to help professionals involve children and young people more in care and protection decisions? A short explanation and application of each of the six core 'qualities and skills' needed in the early stages follows.

Relationship qualities 1: Respect

Respect simply conveys the ability to show that you are 'for' the young person; which is not the same as taking her or his 'side'. The basic idea is the one suggested by the two phrases 'love the child, but dislike the behaviour', and be 'hard on the problem, but soft on the person'. But if we are not careful, we will soon have generated yet another form of rhetoric, the like of which many practitioners say they are growing tired.

A way of understanding how one's own ability to respect others can be put to the test is to think deliberately of people for whom we can find little sympathy and then think how we would demonstrate respect to them. Anti-oppressive practice and the development of equal opportunities are good examples of how language precedes values and attitudes in the hope of changing both. But although we have travelled some way down the road to challenging oppression, how many white people still think that a 'black person is a white person with a black skin' (Egan 1994)?

Respect is a difficult aspect of the relationship to demonstrate but it remains a critical component. It is important, for example, to show that you 'value' a child; but, sometimes, when a child has been ill-treated and abused, s/he is not easy to treasure. Pioneers of the early therapeutic communities in the UK – notably Richard Balbernie at the Cotswold Community, George Lyward at Finchden Manor and A. S. Neill at Summerhill – always stressed that 'stern love', or 'tough love', was what was needed in order to show young people respect. It is still fascinating to note how, when authors write about respect, they soon juxtapose such polarised concepts. Thus they will speak of respect as 'gracious and tough-minded' (Egan 1994), or as offering care in an non-sentimental way. They use language in this way to illustrate why *showing* respect is about demonstrating exactly how we value individuals but in such ways as to help people place demands on themselves. Although they use different words, they convey the same meaning as in the following excerpt from research. When describing what she thought 'partnership in child protection' meant, a parent accused of abusing her child ended up providing us with an eloquent rendition of what it means to show respect: 'It's like the ability to give people bad news while cuddling them at the same time, but without the cuddle masking the bad news.' (Shemmings and Shemmings 1995).

Relationship qualities 2: Genuineness

Being genuine means not hiding behind a role for protection; it involves being a real person with young people. It certainly means never using the kind of 'infantilising' language, or 'diddums-talk', which is impossible to convey in words but readers would no doubt recognise it.

But genuineness does not imply that, as Egan puts it (1994), we are to become 'free spirits, inflicting ourselves on others'. He then refers to the work of other authors and his conclusions contain practical tips for professionals working with young people. First, they should always explain their true purpose and motivation. Secondly, they should try to respond immediately to the child's needs, rather than wait for the right time 'procedurally'. Thirdly, they should always be 'concrete' when talking to children, by avoiding jargon and by conveying complicated ideas clearly to children without being patronising. Finally, professionals who are 'genuine' can, naturally: speak about their own experiences when they are relevant; be vulnerable and show it; talk about 'here and now' thoughts and feelings rather than seeking sanctuary in the 'there and then'; and demonstrate 'congruence' by adopting a 'what-you-see-is-what-you-get' approach but without any abrasiveness.

Relationship qualities 3: Warmth

Already we can see that these qualities are elusive, complex and hard to demonstrate. Is 'warmth' any more straightforward? It seems less complicated but, as we have seen already, its timing might cause children a problem. Whilst I cannot think of any occasion when a practitioner should seek deliberately to be cold and unemotional, there are many children for whom it will be inappropriate to be gushing. Yet this is precisely what one sees in some people, who imply by their verbal and non-verbal behaviour that 'I'm always the life-and-soul-of-the-party, wherever I am or whoever I'm with.' But why, exactly? Lots of people do not like parties; or maybe they have just gone off them for a while. There is nothing more infuriating for some young people than to be with others who insist on jollying everyone else along, preferring the world to be furry and fluffy.

So whilst 'warmth' is a lot easier to get a grip on than 'respect' and 'genuineness', the problem with it is achieving the right balance: too much and the child is suffocated, too little and s/he feels isolated and alone. Egan says that the trick is to be 'warm within reason', yet such a phrase tantalises more than it informs. But he adds to our understanding when he writes: '.... it is ordinarily communicated non-verbally through gestures, posture, tone of voice, touch, and facial expression. Warmth, however, is only one way of showing respect, and not necessarily the best way'. And he then concludes: 'Helpers should be friendly, recognising that the warmth that characterises close friendships is not the same as the facilitative warmth of the helping relationship.'

Relationship skills 1: Attending

As is often the case with skills, we find there are more practical tips on offer. For example, there is Egan's mnemonic SOLER to help us remember what others need in order to feel that we are paying attention to them: we need to be physically *Square(ish)* to the child; s/he will prefer us to adopt an *Open* posture; we should *Lean* towards the child; it is better to maintain some *Eye* contact than to look out of the window or at one's watch; but we need to do all of this in a natural and *Relaxed* way, so as not to be stilted or wooden. Attending properly is actually very easy to understand but extremely difficult to put into practice. We can all remember what it feels like when others have not given us the attention we needed or wanted. It takes time to do it well, but the reward for our patience is young people who will learn to trust us more easily and subsequently become involved in the work more willingly.

Relationship skills 2: Listening

As one would expect, 'listening' goes far beyond the act of 'hearing'. Also, listening involves more than parroting what someone else has said. As Egan points out:

> A tape recorder could do that perfectly. People want more than physical presence in human communication; they want the other person to be present psychologically, socially and emotionally.

Writers in the field of helping and counselling talk about 'active' listening in order to capture this point. Egan, for example, speaks of the need to 'listen actively' for discrepancies between: what people say and what they do; what they think and feel; whether and to what extent their non-verbal behaviour confirms, denies or strengthens their verbal behaviour; and whether the tone of voice used is congruent with what is being said. In the early stages, to be able to listen effectively means being in a position to 'take in' what the person is saying without evaluating it, in the sense of whether what is being said is acceptable or relevant; but this does not exclude the possibility of challenging discrepancies later on, when trust has been developed and strengthened. Finally, Egan stresses the importance of listening to the 'whole person in the context of the social settings of his or her life'.

Relationship skills 3: Empathy

The idea of empathy being the ability to look at someone else's world through *their* eyes has always been contrasted to the more familiar notion of 'sympathy', which is when we look at someone else's world through our *own* lens and from our *own* perspective. But there is more to it than this and, in *The Skilled Helper*, Egan uses the words of Carl Rogers in order to add significantly to the 'standing-in-someone-else's-shoes' definition of empathy:

> It means entering the private perceptual world of the other and becoming thoroughly at home in it. It involves being sensitive, moment by moment, to the changing feelings which flow in this other person, to the fear or rage or tenderness or confusion or whatever that he or she is experiencing. It means temporarily living in the other's life, moving about in it delicately without making judgements.

According to Egan, to be able to demonstrate this immensely complex form of human communication we have to: first, be perceptive to the world of the other person; secondly, possess the know-how to communicate this knowledge; and, thirdly, be assertive and confident enough to overcome our own stage-fright and actually 'do it' – that is, communicate empathically to the other person. Much of the training on empathy revolves around participants trying to respond to co-participants' expressions of emotionally charged thoughts and feelings. To begin with, participants are encouraged to use the, albeit somewhat stilted, formulaic phrase: 'You feel _____ because _____ .' They then try to find their own 'style' to communicate to the other person, which needs to be relaxed, natural and genuine. Egan reminds us in the following example, however, that showing empathy is not always just about words:

I was in the house of a poor family when the father came bursting through the front door shouting 'I got the job!' His wife, without saying a word, went to the refrigerator, got the bottle of beer with a makeshift label on which *CHAMPAGNE* had been written, and offered the bottle to her husband. Beer had never tasted so good.

As stated earlier, differences exist over the extent to which empathy is considered to be a necessary or sufficient condition for future change. For Rogers it was seen as being the core quality and skill around which all others orbit; for Egan and Carkhuff, empathy is seen more as a functional or instrumental part of the whole process of both intra- and inter-personal change. Seen in this light, accurate empathy can promote Egan's goals as follows:

- Build the relationship.
- Stimulate self-exploration.
- Check understandings.
- Provide support.
- Lubricate communication.
- Focus attention.
- Restrain the helper.
- Pave the way.

By 'pave the way' Egan means that empathy can lead into

stronger interventions suggested by the helping model, including challenging a client's assumptions and perceptions, settings goals, formulating strategies, and moving to action.

Conclusion

Part of the purpose of this discussion has been to reinforce a key point in this book: involving children and young people is a matter of artistic judgement. It always has been. 'Caring', 'listening', 'helping', etc. are all higher-order qualities in humans, which cannot be reduced to the 'zeros and ones' needed for processing on the electro-magnetic spectrum. Advanced computers cannot do these things. So, for example, these qualities and skills will not fit into a checklist; neither can we go on a training course to develop *respect, genuineness* and *warmth*. Just saying it sounds silly. But the excitement in all of this is that we are left free to discover in each situation the uniqueness of young people. This may not give much consolation to the busy social worker, who, at the drop of a referral, has to go out and involve young people in enquiries about abuse. But, in a strange way, what may reassure the busy worker who has always believed in the centrality of 'the relationship', is for her or him to know that in terms of gaining the trust and confidence of young people, whatever she or he does, will be a waste of time if she or he forgets these qualities.

Involving children in care and protection is a job that requires creativity, flair, knowledge, skill and judgement; it cannot be done properly if workers rely too heavily on a set of administrative procedures, or on 'skills' to the exclusion of artistry. Or, as Egan put it:

Years ago Rogers .... spoke out against what he called the 'appalling consequences' of an over-emphasis on the micro-skills of helping. Some helper training programmes focus almost exclusively on these skills. As a result, trainers know how to communicate but not how to help.

References

Carkhuff, R. R. and Berenson, B. G. (1967) *Beyond Counselling and Therapy*. New York, NY.: Holt, Reinholt and Winston.

Egan, G. (1994) *The Skilled Helper: A Problem Solving Approach to Helping,* 5th edition. Monterey, Calif.: Brooks-Cole.

Rogers, C. R. (1951) *Client-Centred Therapy*. Boston, Mass.: Houghton-Mifflin.

Shemmings, D. and Shemmings, Y. (1995) 'Defining participative practice in health and welfare' in Jack, R. (ed.) *Empowerment in Community Care*. London: Chapman and Hall.

Shemmings, D. and Shemmings, Y. (1996) 'Building trust with families when making enquiries' in Platt, D. and Shemmings, D. (eds) *Making Enquiries into Alleged Child Abuse and Neglect*. Chichester: John Wiley & Sons.

Shemmings, Y. (1996) *Death, Dying and Residential Care*. Aldershot: Avebury.

CHAPTER 14

CHILD ADVOCACY
Nicky Scutt

The policy of parental participation at child protection conferences has enhanced the overall conduct of the meeting and of its participants. Most importantly it has allowed meaningful discussion and decision-making to take place with parents. However, in professionals' anxiety to ensure that parents are able to participate, sometimes less time and energy has been given to children and young people's participation. This may have resulted in unbalanced conferences in which, other than anecdotally, no one was able to describe the child's views and opinions.

In an attempt to redress this balance West Devon Social Services, the NSPCC, and the Youth Enquiry Service (a local charity) introduced the Child Advocacy Scheme, initially as a six-month pilot project and later permanently.

The aim of the project was to facilitate the participation of children in child protection conferences and to enable their views and opinions to be heard. Mindful of the disempowering effect child protection conferences can have on family members, and that children generally are a disempowered body within the child protection system, those involved in the project believed that to get true participation it was necessary to provide each child with an advocate who was independent from all professional networks and from other family members. All children aged 10 and upwards who are referred for a child protection conference are offered such an advocate. (This age range was chosen because it was felt that younger children are cognitively less likely to participate fully.) Advocates are briefed to explain the child protection conference process to the child or young person, to go through the material that will be presented and to offer the child a range of methods of participation including:

- attending the meeting with their advocate;
- the advocate attending on their behalf;
- sitting behind a two-way mirror;
- the use of audio-tape;
- writing letters.

The advocates are selected from a pool of volunteers already engaged in youth work and counselling within the Youth Enquiry Service. As existing volunteers, they have already received approximately 120 hours of training, including counselling and listening skills. On selection for this scheme they are provided with additional training by the NSPCC on child protection and the conference process.

Some conflicting policies had to be reconciled for this project to become operational. For example, the Youth Enquiry Service operates a total confidentiality policy. This is fundamental to its work and, hence, it felt unable to compromise this principle. Devon Social Services and the NSPCC are charged with the duties and obligations of protecting children from harm and are therefore obliged by law to act on any information where harm is alleged.

The starting point taken was a corporate desire to empower children in the conference process. This was defined as giving children the necessary information and support to enable them to participate meaningfully in this process. It was agreed therefore that for this to be successful it was necessary to invest trust in the young people and to allow them to make decisions concerning any disclosures they may wish to make. After much discussion, it was agreed that the young person's confidentiality would be preserved unless s/he disclosed anything that was life-threatening to her/himself or to another child or young person. This was agreed with the understanding that advocates would advise young people of their rights to protection and counsel them in making disclosures to the relevant authorities.

Evaluation of the pilot project

On completion of the pilot project 22 children (80 per cent) participated within the three districts taking part. This compared very favourably with the previous figure of 20 per cent for the whole West Devon area. Children and young people were interviewed following their participation at the conference. Advocates were interviewed and care managers and the chairperson's views on the service were sought through the use of questionnaires.

The evaluation of the children and young peoples' interviews revealed that, through this scheme, they had gained a clear understanding of the purpose of a conference. Young people felt that preparation was important to helping them to decide how to participate. The majority saw the advocates as their sole source of preparation. They received support from their advocates twice prior to the conference, for about one hour on each occasion.

The young people found the following issues helpful to discuss:

- details about the meeting;
- who would be there, what might be said, what would be decided and what this might mean for them;
- the role of the chairperson;
- what children wanted to say to the meeting and how this could be achieved, and some prepared written statements for the meeting;
- feelings, both about what had happened as well as about attending the meeting;
- practical matters such as a description of the venue, knowing there was a choice about where to sit, and who to sit next to in the meeting;
- the formal and informal 'rules' about the meeting: that is, when to speak, who to speak to, whether they could talk to their advocate, knowing that it is acceptable to sit and listen and not speak, and whether they could leave and return later.

Implications from the project concerning the preparatory stages included the importance of offering young people audience alone without parents or carers present at the meeting. Similarly, the needs of younger children and children with learning difficulties required careful consideration; in particular, they needed more preparation time and in some circumstances the need for specialist advice.

Views of those involved

Forms of participation

The main forms of participation offered were to attend with an advocate or to be represented at the meeting by an advocate. There were no discussions about other forms of participation, for example, the use of audio- or visual-tapes, two-way mirrors, drawings, and so on. The majority said that, even if this had been offered, they would have declined it.

The following reasons were given for not wanting to go:

I was afraid I would be asked something and wouldn't know the answer, and anyway it may be I wouldn't want to answer.

I was embarrassed about hearing what people might say about me.

Talking with my advocate helped me decide not to go as he was going for me and I didn't want to go. It took the pressure off and I didn't feel I needed to go.

Clearly young people had thought about why they did not want to attend. However, these comments raise the question of whether they were given a broad enough range of choices about other forms of participation. Additionally, some were concerned about being made to speak, although this research highlights that those who attended did not feel pressurised to do so. All those involved in child protection conferences, in particular chairpersons and advocates, need to be sensitive to this concern of young people. Young people need to be informed that it is perfectly acceptable to attend and not be heard if that is what they wish.

Those who wanted to attend gave the following reasons:

Better than staying at home while they are all talking about me . . . . I wanted to listen to what they said.

I didn't want to go but even more I didn't want them talking about me behind my back . . . . I wanted to be able to challenge anything I thought was wrong.

They wanted me to be let in on what was going on and they told me I could say anything I wanted, so I thought I should go.

I wanted to go to tell people what I thought and why.

If I wasn't there and we hadn't discussed it, my advocate wouldn't have been able to say anything because she couldn't have said what I thought.

If I thought something was wrong, I could say so. If I'm not there, my advocate can't say because she can't assume what I think.

The young people seemed very clear about why they wanted to be at the meeting, offering a variety of reasons in support. A theme throughout was that the decision to attend was made much easier if they knew that the advocate would be present to support them and speak up for them if it became difficult to do so themselves. However, no young person felt that advocates took over, said too much or spoke without their permission. Young people felt very much in control of how they used their advocates.

All the young people felt that it was right to give them the opportunity to attend the meeting, even if they chose an alternative form of participation. They all felt that it had been their decision whether and how to participate, in consultation with their advocates. None felt pressurised, by professionals, family members or advocates into going (or not going).

At the child protection conference

Although there was evidence that those who attended had a better understanding of the processes and functions of the meeting, both those who attended and those who were represented felt that their contributions had been important from a personal perspective, as well as from the adult's viewpoint. For example:

> They got to hear my views instead of just what the grown-ups think about me and what they think I want.

> They heard both sides [young person and parents] with me being there.

Attenders commented on being nervous initially, in particular about talking in front of a group of adults, and some said they were upset by what they heard. However, this did not appear to detract from their desire to be present. The project suggests that the quality of information shared at the meeting was more accurate as a result of children participating, perhaps for similar reasons as when parents attend – professionals know that they have to substantiate their assessments and reduce jargon and innuendo. Young people felt that the plans were more acceptable as a result of their involvement in devising them together.

None of the young people felt that jargon had been used inappropriately. However, discussions highlighted that many young people did not understand terminology such as 'minutes of the meeting'. Professionals must remain diligent in challenging jargon and cautious about making assumptions about the words they use.

Young people generally were happy with the behaviour of the professionals and family members in the meeting, although they did suggest the following:

- Professionals should ensure that they arrive on time.
- The meeting should start on time.
- The meeting should be restricted to those who work with young people and their families on a regular basis.
- Social work reports should be given to young people before the meeting.
- A less formal atmosphere, with comfortable chairs, tea and biscuits, was preferable to sitting around a table.
- Chairpersons should offer young people a choice about where to sit as they felt their position in relation to other attenders was an important factor.
- Time should be set aside for breaks during lengthy meetings.

- Young people would like copies of the minutes of the meeting, but stress that these should not be sent direct to them as they wanted the opportunity to discuss the contents with an independent adult.
- It is important to ensure that reception staff are both aware of, and sensitive to, the needs of young people attending meetings, and the need for user-friendly waiting areas.

(The last three findings are similar to those made by Yvonne Shemmings earlier in Chapter 4.)

Advocates

Young people valued the fact that the advocates were there for them alone. The independence of the advocates from the formal support systems and from direct knowledge of the family networks and relationships was an important factor in furthering the empowerment of the young people in their chosen method of participation. A number of young people stressed the importance to them of the confidential service offered by advocates, which in their eyes differentiated the advocates from the agencies.

Young people felt that their experience of attendance was enhanced considerably by the support of their advocates, who undertook a variety of tasks within each meeting ranging from support, by 'being there', to talking on the young person's behalf. For example:

> He spoke on my behalf about my thoughts and what I was like. . . . I wouldn't have been able to do that.

> My advocate was the only one in the meeting who was there for *me*.

> Having my own advocate and foster carers there helped me to stay for the whole meeting. If I'd been on my own, I couldn't have coped with what my parents were saying.

The advocate's presence at the meeting was, it seems, an important part of helping young people to undertake the unfamiliar role of child protection conference attender. For those who did not attend, they felt that advocates had put their views across and given them good feedback about what had happened. Although one young person was receiving periodic counselling from her advocate, the remainder had a good grasp of the short-term nature of the advocate's role, all being aware that they could make contact between meetings if they wanted to.

Conclusion

This project is now operating permanently across the Plymouth Districts and many of the points raised from the pilot have been addressed. This was a first attempt to increase social services departments' ability to consult young people who are subject to child protection enquiries. Although some found it difficult and at times distressing, they all wanted to be involved. For some, this was the first occasion on which they had felt consulted, despite the child protection service being primarily concerned about them.

Although this is not the only model of advocacy, it is one that seemed to work for the children and young people concerned. In particular, young people were able to have confidence in their advocate, with much importance being attached to the advocate's independence. Although social workers strive to meet the child's or young person's child protection needs, they do so in the context of children's families and therefore are usually less able to offer either the level of independence necessary or the time to prepare children adequately. (Not surprisingly, perhaps, it was found that the process of preparation took between five and six hours per child.)

Confidentiality proved to be another significant factor for the children and young people. They were able to feel safe with their advocate. To a large degree this was because they knew that only the views they wished to share would be communicated to others. Despite the initial reservations concerning the level of confidentiality offered to the children, this seems to have been a key factor in the empowerment process.

The evaluation identified that other professionals gained a much greater understanding of the issues for the children, thus demonstrating that this is a two-way process. Care managers and chairpersons also voiced their approval of this service and felt that it had enabled a far more balanced conference, with both parents' and children's views being voiced.

Despite their initial trepidation, advocates did not have any difficulty in eliciting agreement from the parents to operate as the children's advocate. The children were then prepared for their conferences and were able to contribute with their advocates' help. Additionally, the standard of the volunteers used for this scheme was extremely high. They all possessed a high level of commitment to, and a strong belief in, the process. They were well trained and well supported by their own agency, and had a strong philosophical base from which to operate.

Both the Children Act 1989 and the 1989 United Nations Convention on the Rights of the Child gave statutory organisations the duty of ensuring that children's views and opinions are both heard and considered when planning for their protection. Children have a right to be heard and understood. This project offered them a mechanism for doing so. Abused children have already suffered. Any subsequent suffering can be reduced by offering them a place in the planning arena in a manner that gives them understanding and allows them to contribute.

CHAPTER 15

USER GROUPS
Dee Lynes, Jim Goddard and Stewart Betts

[In this chapter, all quotations from young people in care are drawn from *The View from the Front: The User View of Child Care in Norfolk* (Lynes and Goddard 1995). All quotations from the Norfolk In-Care Group (NICG) members are drawn from interviews conducted by two of the authors of this chapter with former longstanding and active members of the group.]

User groups for young people with experience of living in care have a short history. The formation of the National Association of Young People in Care (NAYPIC) in 1979 marked their beginning, bringing the views of child care users to the forefront of policy debate during the 1980s and 1990s. Run by and for young people with experience of care systems, NAYPIC sought to rely on the views of its members for its impact.

Today, the *Directory of In-Care and After-Care User Groups in the UK,* (BYPASS/Save the Children 1995) lists 31 currently active user groups. A brief glance through its pages quickly illustrates that they come in all different shapes and sizes. They vary a great deal with respect to such things as the age range of their members, the activities undertaken, the nature of the relationship with their local social services department, the role (if any) of professional adults within the group, and the amount and source of any funding received. Such diversity reflects the localised nature of child care user groups. However, it also renders a strict operational definition of user groups impossible. It makes more sense to define user groups in terms of their broad goals rather than how they seek to achieve them: typically, all child care user groups seek to improve the welfare of young people in care and of those who have already left. Often they offer invaluable support and independent advice for such young people.

User groups can be an important way of ensuring that the views of young people are incorporated in local (and hopefully national) decision-making. Yet despite their many benefits, and the existence of legislation encouraging the development of the user's voice in decision-making, user groups continue to struggle for their survival.

Developing a healthy user group

The development of a healthy user group depends upon two conditions:

1. The user group should meet and represent the needs of the young people in care and care-leavers within its area.
2. The environment in which the user group operates must be conducive to its development.

Thus responsibility for the development of a healthy user group does not rest simply with those young people who choose to organise or join it, but also with the social workers, foster carers and social services managers who influence and shape its surroundings. Both the group and those who affect its environment need to work together to ensure the healthy promotion and survival of the user group.

The nature and purpose of the user group

A user group should seek to represent and work with all users and will need to offer a wide range of services in order to do so. Frequently, user groups are encouraged to provide support to one part of the care population – often those who are dissatisfied for some reason. Representing such young people should, however, only be a part of the group's work. By attracting a broader range of users to the group, it will achieve greater credibility as a representative voice for all young people with experience of the care system, including, for example, those with learning disabilities. This may not always be easy, but it is important to make the attempt whenever possible so that no group is excluded from the type of support that a user group can provide.

The three separate roles of a user group

Our experience indicates that there are three distinctive roles that a user group can have: support group, pressure group and consultative body. The primary role of a user group should always be as a group for young people with experience of life in care. Thereafter, as the group expands and develops, it can act as a pressure group and as a consultative body. Our experience also suggests that a user group must focus on the immediate needs and interests of young people in care, as well as care-leavers, before it begins to tackle anything more ambitious.

Support group

A user group can be a crucial, independent source of support and advice for many young people. This may take the practical form of helping individuals with problems or complaints, supporting them at reviews, helping young people gain access to their files, claiming benefits, or sorting out problems with housing, health and work. However, many young people's needs will be as much 'social' as anything else. Often they simply want the chance to be in touch with other young people in similar situations; to meet and be with others who know what the care experience feels like 'from the inside'. As:

> You could talk to each other and you'll know exactly what each other feels. (Girl, 14, foster care)

> Because it's nice to know what other people's life in care is like too. (Boy, 17, foster care)

During the past decade many local authorities have scaled down residential care in favour of foster placements. Although this shift clearly has helped some young people to move away from the 'in care' identity, others still retain a sense of isolation from those around them. It is therefore a misconception that only those individuals who are dissatisfied with the care they are receiving, or have received, are attracted to user groups. Often, young people who generally are happy with their care also value participation in a user group. This is clear from research into the views of children in care in Norfolk (Lynes and Goddard 1995). Of the 121 young people in care who were surveyed, most were generally satisfied with the care they were receiving. Yet, despite this, 42 per cent said that they would like to be in touch with other young people in care. Many wanted the opportunity to compare and share their care experiences, and to know that they were not alone in the care system.

Clearly, a user group can provide opportunities for such young people to come together and feel less alone. As two members of the NICG put it:

> People could go and talk about their experiences in care and how they're finding life after being in care – you know, that sort of thing; and other people could go and identify and maybe not feel quite so out-of-place in society.

> When I first joined, it was really like a close group. If you didn't have a family – and you weren't going to get a family – that [the NICG] would have been about the next best substitute at that time.

The unique appeal of user groups comes from an understanding that most young people who have been (or who still are) in care can have of the experiences of others. As another NICG member put it:

> Friends that I had that weren't in care I often felt didn't really understand anything that I was going through or, you know, they couldn't really relate to any of it because it was right out of their norm. I often think friends and people outside the care system used to judge me and there was this big stigma, whereas inside the group everybody's equal – nobody's better than anybody else. There's just a lot of empathy there.

Many young people benefit personally from belonging to a user group, through making new friends and doing something that they feel is worthwhile. The following quotations, from previous NICG members, illustrate this:

> I stayed with it because it was really positive, it was good fun, it was nice to meet other people, to share experiences.

> I suppose it was the most positive, interesting thing I was doing at the time. Everything else I was doing at that time wasn't that good. It wasn't stuff that made me feel good about myself.

> Some people got to talk about things they hadn't talked about before . . . . There was that emphasis on talking and listening.

Joining a new group and meeting new people can be a daunting prospect and allowance needs to be made for this. Consideration needs to be given to the age, mobility and literacy of potential members. A range of opportunities to make contact with the group must be provided so that young people can choose a way that they feel comfortable with. These opportunities can range from receiving an informative and regular newsletter to attending meetings and helping to run the group. In the case of the NICG, young people took much more interest in the monthly newsletter than they did in attending formal meetings.

Pressure group

When it acts as a support group, a user group can advocate on behalf of an individual (for example, by attending reviews or helping a young person make a complaint). However, in a pressure group role the user group advocates for improvement in the quality of their lives on behalf of young people in care and care-leavers as a group – whose members decide their own agenda of issues that need to be addressed.

Frequently, this role as pressure group will bring the group into direct contact with its local authority. In doing so it can help to keep the local authority informed about the developing needs and wishes of the young people it represents. Thus, it can play an important role in quality assurance. In its campaigning role the user group also helps to develop the organised voice of young people in care and care-leavers. Alongside other organisations, it may adopt a more educational role. For example, NICG members regularly speak to social work students at the nearby college of further education, as well as at the local university, about what it was like to be brought up in care:

> Personally, I think where the NICG made most effect was by going to speak to social work students and people that worked in social services . . . . because it's very hard to change social services from the outside. I think it needs to be changed from the inside really . . . . What we told them wasn't all that disastrous – it was probably quite standard but they were really freaked out by it. (NICG member)

Consultative body

Finally, a user group can act as a consultative body – in effect, as partners working together. In this role it agrees to discuss issues raised by those outside the group on matters that affect the lives of the young people it represents. For example, a local authority may see the user group as a vehicle for consulting users when setting policy or designing information leaflets, etc., but it is important that this does not become a burden imposed upon the group; there should be a request that a user group be used in a consultative capacity.

The environment of the user group

The environment in which a user group develops is determined to a large extent by those people and agencies with whom the group interacts. Since most user groups operate within local authority boundaries, clearly the local authority and its employees (and carers) have a major influence on shaping this environment. Voluntary sector agencies can also help to create an environment that actively promotes a user group developing; or they can hinder its progress.

Policies, practices and attitudes

Unfortunately, even when senior managers try to promote the development of user groups, staff attitudes are at best lukewarm. Inability to be proactive amongst grassroots staff renders such a positive management approach largely ineffective. Some staff and carers can feel threatened by what they see as a potential source of criticism and can either knowingly prevent information getting to young people or fail to give it the priority it deserves. The NICG encountered some individual social workers and carers who were genuinely supportive; but many were not helpful and some were actively hostile. This experience is not uncommon amongst user groups.

The need for personal accountability

There is a pressing need for greater personal accountability amongst both social workers and carers, so that decisions as to whether or not information about local user groups is passed on are not left to personal discretion. Negative attitudes at an individual level have a powerfully detrimental effect on the survival chances of a user group, and a departmental mechanism to counteract such effects is necessary if any meaningful development is to take place.

Developing a culture of constructive criticism

Social services departments should encourage a culture of constructive criticism. If staff and carers are unable to accept criticism from each other about their practices, then they are likely to remain resistant to the idea of a user group having an active pressure-group role. The development of a positive culture may take some time, but ultimately it can lead to staff and carers feeling less threatened by a user group that develops an active pressure-group role.

Appropriate support: source and type

Although often done with good intentions, many local authorities mistakenly think that in order to empower a group they need to adopt a hands-off approach. Also, some user groups believe that they should survive without local authority support, or that such support will always threaten their independence. This is not necessarily true. Of the 65 care-leavers who took part in the NICG research, 75 per cent said that they preferred after-care support to be provided by social services rather than by any other agency. Furthermore, the majority of young people in care were happy with their relationship with social services. Clearly, most young people in care do not have as difficult a relationship with social services as is often assumed and, in addition, even those care-leavers who had experienced difficulties when leaving care still preferred to have regular support from social services. This suggests that the practice of contracting out support of user groups to outside agencies in the belief that young people will respond to an 'independent' agency in preference to social services is unfounded.

Many user groups struggle with the basic administrative tasks that all groups demand. It is in this and other related areas that a constructive working relationship with the local authority proves to be most helpful. Often, support could more appropriately be given in kind rather than in purely financial terms. If the local authority can provide appropriate administrative and financial management support, this relieves a lot of organisational pressure from the group.

Recruitment

Where a user group exists, membership should be a choice available to all young people who are in or have left care. However, because of confidentiality constraints, the local authority is the only organisation that can ensure that all young people get information about the group to enable them to make this choice. Relying on individual social workers and carers to pass on information tends not to work. When Norfolk Social Services Department organised direct access to young people (so that research questionnaires could be distributed), over 40 new members were recruited in one month. Clearly, access to direct mailing is essential. Without this, less effective publicity, such as poster campaigns, leaflet distribution and local advertisements, usually only result in user groups continuing to be made up of a small (and potentially unrepresentative) number of young people.

Time and expectations: whose needs are being met?

Finally, a local authority may expect too much of a user group too soon or, indeed, look for concrete benefits to justify giving it scarce resources. However, a user group is there to meet the needs of young people in care and care-leavers, not those of the local authority. The latter must be patient and recognise that the primary role of a user group is as a support group. Thereafter, gradually it can develop into a pressure group and offer a consultative role. Time (usually years rather than months) needs to be given to allow the group to develop an identity. Without this important stage, the group is prone to collapse.

Conclusion

We have tried to demonstrate the importance of user groups. If user groups are to become a stable and integral part of local child care decision-making, careful nurturing is required, both by those within the group and by those who shape its environment. Only such careful nurturing will enable user groups to achieve their potential.

References

Lynes, D. and Goddard, J. (1995) *The Review from the Front: The User View of Child Care in Norfolk.* Norwich: Norfolk Social Services Department.

Patel, S. (1995) *Directory of In-Care and After-Care User Groups in the UK.* London: BYPASS/Save the Children.

CHAPTER 16

PREPARING CHILDREN FOR INVOLVEMENT IN DECISION-MAKING

Alison Corner, Catherine Rushforth and David Shemmings

Imagine you have just learned that you have a sister who lives abroad. She is due to arrive at the airport tomorrow. You have never met her. Indeed, up until this point you did not even know you had a sister. It came as a complete shock when you found out because you had always thought you were an 'only child'. At the precise moment when you were told the news you were flabbergasted . . . . and thrilled. After a couple of hours and a stiff drink (or two!) you begin to think 'I want to meet her, but how do I prepare myself for this?' What might go through your mind?

Naturally, everyone would think about the encounter at the airport in different ways. To begin with, although some patterns would be discernible for us among the inevitable cascade of feelings and questions, intuitively we would be distinguishing between the more practical features of the meeting and its emotional content. It seems that most human beings in situations when plans and preparations need to be made will make similar distinctions.

The *practical aspects* will consist of questions such as: Which terminal at the airport? What time train do I need to catch? Shall I drive instead; is my car reliable enough? How will I recognise her? Should I go on my own? On the other hand, those concerning the more *emotional aspects* of the meeting will include: How will I feel when we meet? Will we get on with each other? Should she stay at a hotel, or at home with me/us? And, of course, it will not be long (if indeed it was not one of the first questions to spring to mind) before you start to wonder why no one told you that you had a sister. Perhaps those who could have told you are no longer around (or maybe you never knew them anyway). Perhaps they did not know either. Either way, you are going to experience a whole host of feelings in a short space of time.

As an adult, you would probably deal with these practicalities and feelings by discussing and negotiating them with your sister. Before talking to her, you may well have attempted to order your own thoughts by talking them through with friends, your partner or other supportive people. As a self-protective mechanism, you might begin to consider any contingency plans you might want to employ, such as 'What will I do if we are very different from each other?'

Meeting a birth relative highlights situations whereby adult-to-adult interactions assume a balance of power by virtue of age, joint experiences, and motivations or common goals. However, in other adult-to-adult situations we may not feel that we have the same balance of power. For instance, you may have visited your doctor with the aim of seeking some form of treatment or advice. If, during your consultation, you found your doctor to be unsympathetic and felt s/he failed to respond as you would have wished, you might have considered the options available to you to redress this situation. For instance you might seek a second opinion, choose to change your doctor, pursue a homeopathic remedy, or make a complaint.

The point is that in many situations in which adults are dissatisfied with services they receive, they are often able to make use of alternative ways of redressing the power imbalance until they are more satisfied with the service.

Unfortunately, young people and their families involved in family support and child protection processes do not feel that they have the same kinds of options; thus we need to consider how we can empower them to become participants from the outset. Young people seem acutely aware of the need to be prepared emotionally for these situations – and of ways in which the problems they experienced could have been overcome – as the following excerpts from recent research into the involvement of young people in child protection conferences illustrate (Shemmings 1996):

> Some of the things they said brought back bad memories. I suppose it couldn't have been handled any differently – it's got to come out. But if it was a child's first meeting, then they ought to be warned what it would be like, so that she can decide or he can decide whether they want to go to it or not, or whether they want to be included if certain things come up. If the child feels uncomfortable in the meeting, they should be able to leave the room or at least be warned that it might happen. The worse thing would be that the child had to sit through something painful because they did not know about it.

> I think it's good to be there but it depends on what kind of person you are – whether you can take it – because if you are going to hear what all those people are saying about you, and this makes you upset, there is no point in being there.

Although, as has been noted in the introduction to this book, there is little research currently available concerning the involvement of children, what does exist confirms the need to address the emotional aspects of the meeting when preparing a child or young person.

Preparation, which includes the emotional and practical aspects of the meeting, will empower the young person to make an informed decision as to how s/he wants to be involved in the process. How might this be addressed? Again we consider it important to distinguish two different aspects of preparation: the practical and the emotional.

Preparing the young person practically

The key question that you as a worker need to answer when considering the involvement of a young person in a family support or child protection process is 'Is this young person of sufficient age and understanding?' In order to do so, you will need to clarify the following:

- Consider the developmental stage of the young person; that is, would the young person be able to listen to and understand information shared at the meeting?
- Consider the purpose and focus of the meeting. Is it appropriate for the young person to be involved? For instance, if the meeting is about future plans for the child, including an assessment of needs and risks, and it is thought that the young person is developmentally at a stage that s/he could contribute to this process, it is likely to be appropriate for the

young person to attend. However, if the meeting is about funding decisions, or complex legal matters, it may be inappropriate to invite the young person.
- As with preparation for all meetings, consideration should be given to the individual needs of family members to participate actively in the meeting: for example, regarding wheelchair access, literacy, translation and interpretation services, hearing loops, child care arrangements, waiting facilities, refreshments, etc.
- You will need to be clear about how this meeting fits in with the overall process that the child is involved in, because this is crucial. For instance, a young person might be subject to children 'looked after' processes and reviews as well as child protection processes and conferences. If *you* are not clear about the differences in purpose, focus and decision-making powers of these meetings, you will find it difficult to explain this to a young person.
- You will also need to know how the meeting will be managed. For example, what is the chairperson's style? Is there a set format or agenda for the meeting? Are there any exclusion criteria? Does the chairperson meet with family members before the meeting?

Preparing the young person emotionally

It is important that you discuss with the young person the possible emotional implications of attending the meeting. You will need to assist the young person to understand their role and contribution within the meeting, and the emotional issues this may raise for them. Equally, you will need to be very clear about your own role in relation to the young person at the meeting, and the type of information you might be sharing. For instance, you may be the allocated social worker for *the family*, thus you are not there as the young person's advocate, although you may be sharing her or his views as you understand them but alongside the views of other family members.

Explore the possibilities of how the young person might feel when attending the meeting. It is helpful to assist the young person to imagine many of the different scenarios that might arise, and rehearse ways of managing this. For instance, a young person might explore ways of coping with a parent's anger in the meeting in order to feel reasonably confident, after rehearsing her or his response, that should the situation arise, s/he could cope.

It is helpful to consider with the young person typical *best- and worst-case scenarios*. Inexperienced professionals sometimes shy away from 'worst case' scenarios for fear of worrying the young person. However, it is unlikely that this experience will be any worse than those that led to the young person's involvement with social services.

Relaying the views of the young person

One of the striking results that emerged from the research into children's involvement in child protection conferences (Shemmings 1996; and Chapter 5) is that they were very clear in their minds that *being involved* did not necessarily mean being in the room. As one child put it:

> I like to know what's going to happen in the meeting. If there's lots of problems at the meeting . . . . and if it's too pressurising, then I wouldn't want to go . . . . I'd get someone else to go and talk for me.

Others interviewed in the research spoke in a similar vein:

> If the child didn't want to come to the meeting, then they shouldn't be made to. Someone else could say it or it could be written down.

> The only good opportunity of being there is hearing what others say and being able to say something if what they say is incorrect – so you could stick up for yourself.

> If I wanted to say something I should have been in another room, or get my social worker to say it for me, or write things on paper and get my social worker to read it out.

The model of participation outlined briefly in Chapter 5 – and explained in more detail in Shemmings (1998) – can be used not only to help children decide how they want to participate in the meeting but also to relay their views to the conference if they prefer not to be in the room.

Debriefing young people after meetings

As stated in the Introduction to this book, one of the young people in the research (Shemmings 1996) said that she did not think her mother should have been offered a cup of coffee in the child protection conference. As we saw earlier, she went on to give her reasons:

> She abuses me. I thought they were all going to tell her to stop hitting me all the time; but no, not only do they not tell her off, they're all nice to her and she gets offered a cup of coffee.

We can all sympathise with her, but this excerpt demonstrates powerfully the importance of helping the young person appreciate what the meeting does and does not do. This obviously had not happened in the above excerpt because the young person expected her mother to be pilloried at the conference. Consequently, a series of debriefing questions should be discussed as soon after the meeting as is practically possible. This is to try and ensure that the young person has not misunderstood the decisions made, and that s/he can talk about any feelings that have been rekindled as a result of the meeting. Remember, just because you attended the same meeting, you cannot assume that everyone else present, heard, understood and assimilated information in the same way as you. The aim of the debriefing process is to clarify with the young person:

- what s/he has heard;
- how s/he understands it and the decisions made;
- the emotional impact of the meeting on the young person.

Ideally, the person conducting the debriefing process with the young person should be the same person who was engaged in the preparation process.

Conclusion

To return to the meeting at the airport: now that we have tried to think through what might happen and how we might feel, in what sense are we 'better prepared'? Might we not have spoiled something by being so logical and calculating? It is at this point that the similarity between the two events breaks down. Meeting one's sister is likely to be an exciting event; going to a meeting about family support or child protection is not.

Good actors know that to perform well they need to know their lines, their cues and how to read and respond to an audience. The point about being better prepared is to be in a position to minimise surprise and thereby recapture the locus of control. This is the main purpose of preparing young people for meetings. Done well, it empowers them by minimising the unexpected and it helps them to express their own wishes and feelings. The extent to which the adults then listen and take any notice will determine whether the young person believes it was worth it or not.

References

Shemmings, D. (1996) *Involving Children in Child Protection Conferences.* Social Work Monographs, No.152, Norwich: University of East Anglia.

Shemmings, D. (1998) *In On the Act: Involving Children in Family Support and Child Protection – A Training Pack for Professionals.* Norwich: University of East Anglia.

CHAPTER 17

PROFESSIONAL SUPPORTERS AND CHILDREN'S INVOLVEMENT
Alison Corner

Why is it that some children and their families are not adequately informed or involved in family support and child protection processes? I do not believe workers intend deliberately to create unsatisfactory working relationships or withhold information from family members. Rather, workers who are not themselves clear or certain about their own and others' roles and responsibilities in specific child care processes will not be in a position confidently to seek, explain or share clear and coherent information with children and their families.

This raises the issue of supervision and training available to staff. Experience reinforces the importance of this in influencing positive outcomes for children. However, the quality of supervision and professional support for workers is often variable and in some cases lacking. Poor support leads to uncertainty and lack of confidence amongst practitioners, which, in turn, affects the family members involved.

In this chapter I have defined 'professional supporters' as those with supervisory, managerial, consultative or advisory responsibilities with front-line workers. I now look more closely at why supporters are required to undertake this role and how they might proactively encourage workers to involve children in child care processes by means of the following questions:

- Who is a professional supporter and why does s/he have a responsibility to undertake this role?
- What does this responsibility entail?
- How might supporters tackle the responsibilities in practice?

These questions are more fully discussed below.

The professional supporter

In its simplest form the supervisory or management role concerns the management and observation of a worker's performance in carrying out the job in question whilst offering the necessary support to do so. Support and advice is also available through consultancy, usually from workers with expertise in specialist areas. For instance, independent chairpeople (most often associated with reviews for children 'looked after' or child protection conferences) have skills and specialist knowledge in their respective fields. They will often provide consultation to workers within the agency in these areas of work. Consultation in its simplest form refers to the provision of objective advice, information and assistance to a worker.

The responsibilities

Often the consultation and supervisory responsibilities are interlinked within agencies. For instance, consultation usually forms part of the supervisory process, although it might also be sought outside this relationship. The way in which the supervisor's role differs from the consultant's concerns the authority given by the agency for the supervisor to direct the worker, leaving the value of the consultant's role as that of impartiality and independence.

Although some responsibilities for supporting workers will differ according to role boundaries, there are important areas of overlap in the supervisory, consultative and chairperson roles. This includes the responsibility to support workers by *providing relevant knowledge* that enhances the workers' abilities to develop their own practice and skills needed to do the job. It also includes the responsibility to *monitor the appropriateness and effectiveness of the work undertaken* with the child. Gadsby-Waters (1992) has defined this as:

> Clarifying the direction the work needs to take, assisting the worker to develop an awareness and insight into how his or her opinions, attitudes and biases affect, or not, the intervention.

Tackling responsibilities – providing a framework

There is little doubt that professional supporters are working in a fast and ever-changing environment requiring constant acquisition of new knowledge and skills to meet these challenges. However, managers often say that they feel unprepared for their current jobs. With this in mind, I have endeavoured to provide a framework that identifies specific areas that professional supporters need to address if children and young people are to be involved positively in child care processes.

The framework I find most helpful derives from anti-discriminatory practice and includes four components: *knowledge, values, skills* and *experience*. By modifying these four components, I have attempted to focus specifically on issues affecting the involvement of children and young people.

Knowledge

An important starting point is to access knowledge about the historical and contemporary versions of childhood. Professional supporters require an understanding of the contemporary view of childhood and how this has perpetuated itself through legislation and statutory responsibilities of welfare organisations.

Implicit in any work with children and their families is the need for workers to locate a child's experience in her or his own context. Thus, issues such as race, gender, disability, class and age must be identified. Proper weight and consideration needs to be given to the way in which the child and family's context strengthens or negatively affects the child's life experiences. To do this, professional supporters and workers require knowledge both of universal forms of discrimination and of specific types of anti-discriminatory activity (such as anti-racist or anti-sexist practice). A failure to understand these issues can result in professional practice that reinforces negative and discriminatory messages that children may already have experienced in society.

Working with children requires knowledge about 'usual' child development – how the child's understanding and perceptions of people in the world will vary with their age and experience. Coupled with this is the need for knowledge about the principles of good communication in general, but with children specifically.

Individually, children will have varying needs and requirements, depending on their circumstances. For instance, work with a child who has communication difficulties will need to be underpinned by knowledge of alternative methods of communication. Likewise, an awareness of the possible effects of traumatic experiences on the development of the child is important in order that the communication techniques used are gauged appropriately for the child.

Clearly, all professional supporters and workers need to be familiar with any policies, procedures and practice guidance informing child care practices, as well as with research findings. Senior managers have a responsibility to sanction, own and disseminate these throughout their organisation. Training should highlight these policies and guidance.

Values

As has been said, an important support function is to assist workers to develop an awareness into how their own opinions, attitudes and biases affect their interventions with children and families. Morrison (1993) explored this:

> Difference is a constant reality in supervision, whether it arises in terms of gender, race, age, disability, sexual orientation, class, religion or nationality. And yet many supervisors struggle with how to put it on the agenda in a constructive and proactive way.

Professional supporters need to be clear about their own value base through the acquisition of knowledge about versions of childhood. It is likely that both the professional supporter and worker will have begun to identify and examine their own value base in relation to children. This in itself is important and needs to be taken further so that both the supporter and the worker are able explicitly to share their value base and consider how this might influence any work with children. For instance, the supporter will both be interested to find out how the worker translates specific values about the involvement of children into action and to ask for evidence of this.

An exploration of values can assist professional supporters gauge how motivated a worker actually is to involve children. This is important, as supporters have a responsibility on behalf of the child to be sure that appropriate steps have been taken to assess the child's ability to be involved in the process and then actively to prepare them to do so.

Professional supporters need to demonstrate their ability to translate the value of positively involving children. For instance, if we take the example of the chairperson, is the language used in information packs and other correspondence sent to children and young people before and after meetings appropriate and helpful? Similarly, the way in which the chairperson manages the sharing of information and language (especially professional jargon) during the meeting will provide evidence of her or his value base. Chairpersons who are committed to supporting young people will take steps to ensure that the child has been prepared properly. This could be demonstrated in a variety of ways. For example, the chairperson might arrange always to discuss how a child has been prepared for involvement in a meeting with the front-line worker and supervisor; then she or he can check whether the child is clear about the purpose of the meeting, discuss how it will be run, and ask whether there are any questions or issues that the child wants clarified.

Chairpersons committed to involving children will also evidence this by ensuring that children's needs and requirements regarding race, culture, gender, language, age and disability, and their preferred method of involvement, are considered prior to the meeting and addressed within it.

Skills

There are some skills that are specific to involving children. For example, workers need to communicate with children within the child's developmental stage. This might include working with interpreters for children who do not have English as a first language or who have some form of sensory or speech impairment. The acquisition of these skills is important for chairpersons of meetings.

If the worker has the knowledge and appropriate value base to empower children to be involved in the process, then skill development is something that can be learned though training or through supervision and consultancy.

Techniques for communication should be appropriate for the individual child, and supporters need to check that workers feel confident and comfortable with such chosen techniques.

In terms of assessment skills, the worker involved with a child who has experienced trauma will need to assess its extent by liaising with professionals and family members who have information about the child's preferred method of communication, or by observing the child, before deciding which techniques would be most helpful in these circumstances.

Experience

The term 'experience' refers to both the past and the present. It can be helpful for professional supporters to identify what are their own experiences in working with children in decision-making processes and then to assist the worker to do the same.

Reflecting on current practice in a constructive way plays an important part in determining the effectiveness of interventions. Feedback might also be sought from others involved in the process (for instance the child, the family and other professionals) as a way of improving practice.

Using the example of the chairperson again, s/he also requires feedback about her or his chairing skills and general management of the meeting. Views can be sought from both family members and professionals about their experience of the meeting, what they found helpful and what might have been more helpful to them in terms of the chairperson's management of the meeting.

Conclusion

A model of supervision and consultation, based upon an anti-discriminatory perspective, has been applied to the involvement of young people in family support and child protection processes. It is argued that this can provide professionals with the support and guidance that they need to help family members participate.

References

Gadsby-Waters, J. (1992) *The Supervision of Child Protection Work.* Aldershot: Avebury.

Morrison, T. (1993) *Staff Supervision in Social Care.* London: Longman.

CHAPTER 18

USING PROFESSIONAL JUDGEMENT
Catherine Kenney

This chapter aims to help the practitioner to interpret children's verbal and non-verbal communication within the context of their life experiences. It will also explore factors that may inhibit children being able to retell what they need or want to say. The case examples used mainly consider issues regarding child protection, but the principles equally apply to children who are looked after or who are in need. (The first names of the children referred to in the examples are fictitious.)

Factors to take into account when interpreting a child's communication

How was the child's story obtained?

Children are more likely to be able to say what they need to say if they are relaxed and have confidence in the competency of the adult with whom they are communicating. Closed and direct questioning is less likely to enable a child to explain the complexity and entirety of her or his wishes and feelings than a more open and exploratory approach. Young children may need the help of toys, pictures, paints, etc., to help them to report. Reliance on verbal communication alone from a young child is more likely to lead to misunderstandings of the child's position. An interpretation of the child's situation is more likely to be valid if the information has come from multiple sources such as observation of the child's behaviour, parental accounts of the child, and the child's verbal account.

Children are more able to communicate accurately in their first language. It is essential, therefore, that when young children are asked to recount difficult incidents or to explain their wishes and feelings, they are enabled to do this in the language of their choice, thereby maximising their opportunity to recount the details and subtleties of their position.

Where was the child's story ascertained?

Children are more likely to be relaxed and able to communicate freely in a familiar or child-centred setting. However, social workers often need to talk to children in settings that may not maximise the child's ability to be relaxed, such as schools, video suites or social service offices. For example, nervous children who need to be transported to a video suite, equipped as such suites are with unfamiliar technology, are less likely to be able to tell their story than children who can be spoken with in familiar surroundings. For some children, however, talking in their home may be an inhibitor. A child who is having difficulties in the foster placement, for example, may worry about the potential repercussions of voicing difficulties if the foster carer is present or can overhear. This child would need some guidance or advice about how any worries should be voiced effectively.

Children of any age are more likely to be able to explain their situation, wishes and feelings accurately if asked to do so outside a meeting or formal structure. In practice, this means that the child's account of events, or their wishes and feelings, must have been canvassed prior to any meeting and the means of the child's account being presented to the meeting agreed with the child.

Who has ascertained the child's story?

Generally, children are able to speak more freely with adults with whom they are familiar. Being in the presence of parents or other adults who are trusted by the child may help her or him feel safe enough to say what s/he needs. In social work this is not always appropriate or possible. Care needs to be taken because these very people may inhibit the child, as they may be afraid of the consequences for the adult of what the child may say.

The relationship between the child and the adult to whom they are speaking is an important factor, which will determine what the child will say. Children are aware that adults have more power than they. Individual children will also recognise that adults in particular roles, such as teachers, social workers or the police, will have differing degrees of authority over them and differing significance for them. For some children, for example, teachers may represent authority to a child to such an extent that s/he may not be able to discuss emotional issues with them. A child's perception of police officers may be as helpful community members whom they can trust, or they may be seen as an authority that puts people who have done something wrong in prison; children holding the latter view will find it hard to communicate freely as they may have an overriding fear of being put in prison, or causing somebody else to go to prison. Social workers, foster carers and parents will all be seen differently by individual children.

Other power differentials include gender, race, class and other 'aspects of difference'. In some cases these may become a significant block to a child being able to speak freely. For example, an Indian Muslim girl is more likely to be able to say what she needs to say to an Indian Muslim woman than to an Indian Hindi man. Similarly, children who have been abused may have difficulties speaking freely with a person of the same gender or race as the abuser, as they may reflect the imbalance of power experienced by the child at the time of the abuse. It is important, therefore, to take the child's life experience into account before deciding who should speak with the child.

If the adult and the child are from different cultures, it is important that the adult is aware of any potential to misinterpret verbal or non-verbal communication from the child. Non-verbal communication is particularly open to misinterpretation. For example, a child may be silent because in her or his culture it is seen as good manners, but the adult may perceive the silence as a sign of low intelligence or surly behaviour. Eye contact from Asian girls might be interpreted as bold and insolent within their own culture, whilst an absence of eye contact may be seen by a white European person as evasive, or a sign of a child who is withdrawn or lacking in self-confidence.

Children from racial minorities will have experienced racism or will be aware of family and friends who have experienced racism. This life experience may be a block to these children, preventing them from feeling comfortable to speak freely about sensitive issues with adults from the majority racial group.

Was the child in crisis?

A crisis may precipitate children being able to speak of life events that they would usually choose not to describe. Their usual means of dealing with life may have been overwhelmed temporarily to the point where they decide that they need to share their anxieties. An example of this from my own experience involved a 15-year-old girl who had experienced regular beatings and verbal degradation from her stepfather for several years. This only came to social services' notice when she went to stay with an adult friend after being severely injured. Realising that she enjoyed feeling safe, she recognised that the only way to maintain her position away from her stepfather was to recount her experiences of abuse.

The need to tell may only last for a very short time because the child may be attempting to accommodate her or his immediate feeling of being overwhelmed and may psychologically redefine the crisis in order to deal with its implications. A child who has been physically harmed, for example, can move quickly from a feeling of injustice and indignation to feeling that the incident was insignificant and that they deserved the abuse. This reframing helps the child not to have to accept the implications of being abused and what that might mean about their relationship with the abuser. It is essential, therefore, that if the child says s/he needs to talk, the moment is not lost. Skilled practitioners will recognise when they need to respond immediately to a child.

It is also important to recognise that a child's wishes and feelings stated at a crisis point may reflect a temporary means of resolving the crisis or reducing the current level of fear, rather than longer term wishes and feelings. An example of this involved two sisters, Shelley and Emily, who lived within an emotionally and physically abusive family. When they were both subject to extreme physical abuse, their normally conflictual relationship changed temporarily to a supportive one. They both left the family home, made a statement to the police, and both stated that they did not want ever to see their mother again. Both girls were eventually able to see their mother when they were convinced of their safety. Their message was not, in effect, that they did not want ever to see or be with their mother; rather, they had an immediate need to be safe and for other people to know of their problems.

Children in crisis are less likely to describe their situation verbally. They may regress and communicate their distress through their behaviour, such as wetting, soiling, aggression or withdrawing. Children who communicate using a second language may find that their fluency in their second language is reduced through stress. This has implications for children who use sign language, Makaton, Blissboards, or whose first spoken language is not that of the majority of the population.

To what extent is the child able to comprehend and predict the consequences of what s/he says?

It is important to recognise that most children infrequently need to consider carefully the consequences of what they say they want or the consequences of describing significant life events. For children who have been harmed or who are looked after by social services, this becomes an important skill. Some children's life experiences may be so limiting that they are unable to imagine what they would like to happen, or they may be so fearful that they cannot communicate what has happened. A child who has suffered long-term emotional cruelty, who has been consistently ridiculed and given the message that they are unlovable is unlikely to perceive that this situation could change. An abused child may have developed distorted reasoning and may have become unable to work out logically what might be the consequences of what they say they want. An example of this can be seen in the case of Kate and Mary, who were told constantly by their mother that if they *truly* loved her then they would agree to short-term fostering to give her a break. When they did agree to this, they were then blamed for causing separation and leaving their mother. This pattern of putting the girls in a double-bind over several years resulted in them losing confidence in identifying their own feelings, because they were unable to predict the outcome if their wishes and feelings were granted.

Similarly, a child who has experienced gross inconsistency will develop an inability to predict outcomes. Christopher, aged 8, would experience being praised for using his initiative one day and the next day would be blamed and shouted at for doing the same thing (such as running the bath). House rules changed daily, without warning and without logic. Eventually Christopher became watchful and nervous. He rarely acted spontaneously or spoke without being invited to do so, because he was unable to predict the outcome of his actions.

A skilled professional will be able to recognise that some children are not able to predict the consequences of what they say and will take special care to ensure that the child understands what may happen about what they have said. Conversely, other young people may understand only too well what may happen and will have to make choices about telling other people about their circumstances.

How emotionally 'free' is the child to communicate?

Children communicate most accurately when they are relaxed and communicating freely about something that does not threaten the stability of their world, their means of coping with it, or their primary attachments. Social workers frequently need to talk with children about issues that threaten all of these.

Children (and adults) find it more difficult to communicate freely if they have to defend their vulnerabilities. This can be seen on a day-to-day level with children whose misbehaviour has been exposed. A normally bright and open child quickly can become uncommunicative, surly and belligerent, as s/he tries to ward off rebuke. Children who are known within social services settings are more vulnerable than other children and therefore are more likely to be reticent when talking about their difficulties.

Abused children will have found means of defending themselves psychologically from the effects of the abuse. These ways of coping may become dysfunctional in the long term. It is important, however, to respect the child's means of surviving. This may result in the child not feeling free to discuss a range of topics that they think might threaten their survival. It may be that children need to have explored all the consequences for themselves before they are able to discuss the abuse. They may not be accurate in these predictions, but it is important to acknowledge that children possess their own wisdom when deciding whether to discuss abusive life experiences. Even if asked directly, some children deny that they have been abused because they do not yet feel safe enough to expose their feelings. This can be particularly frustrating when workers are confident that a child is suffering ill-treatment but does not say so when given the opportunity – and it may compromise the worker's capacity to intervene and try to prevent further ill-treatment.

A worker may be aware of factors that could be silencing the child. Children may feel reassured if the worker voices her or his awareness of what might be keeping the child quiet and if she or he then explains the potential consequences to the child. This was illustrated powerfully by an 11-year-old girl, Charlotte. The social worker had been told by a number of children that, along with them, Charlotte was being abused by an older man. In describing the abuse, the other children also said that the eldest girl (aged 16) introduced them to the man and had made threats to them to ensure that they did not tell about the abuse. The workers heard that Charlotte's mother had previously visited the man herself, for sex (but did not know of his abuse of Charlotte), and furthermore that the 16-year-old girl had stripped Charlotte and then put her down a manhole. Predictably Charlotte did not allege abuse when interviewed. The worker considered that Charlotte could be being psychologically silenced by a number of factors:

- She did not want to involve her mother in any allegations.
- She was afraid of having done something wrong as she had accepted small amounts of money from the abuser.
- She did not want to implicate her friends and did not know that they had chosen to speak.
- She was afraid of the 16-year-old girl.

The worker talked with Charlotte's parents and asked them to reassure Charlotte that they would support her if she did need to say anything. The worker also explained about confidentiality to Charlotte and spoke in hypothetical terms to her about what children are sometimes afraid of when they are interviewed, including issues of guilt and fear of others. Charlotte chose at that point to tell her parents what had happened to her by writing it down. She was also able to describe what she was afraid of and was reassured about this.

Emotionally harmed children may struggle with the idea of being able to tell their story or to portray their wishes or feelings. Children may have learnt to cope with emotional maltreatment by cutting themselves off from their feelings, leaving them emotionally 'flat'. They may not be able to experience or name emotions. These children are both psychologically threatened and puzzled by questions that expect them to 'explore their feelings'.

Children who have been put in a 'double bind', as in the case of Kate and Mary described above, and other children who have learnt that they must put their parents needs and feelings first, will have difficulty identifying their own needs and feelings because they will have experienced negative feedback in the past. An extreme example of this is the experience of a 15-year-old girl who had been expected to care for her mother for many years. Her mother had criticised her when she had attended therapy alone, saying 'I had to find another child to cuddle because you weren't here.' This young girl learnt that, if she separated from her mother and put her own (developmentally appropriate) needs first, her mother would respond either by severe rejection, which sometimes involved the child being looked after by foster carers, or by extreme attention-seeking behaviour, such as self-harming. The parent's behaviour resulted in the child being unable to identify her own needs independently from her need for her mother to be safe.

Children who constantly are needing to battle to maintain their place in the family will not feel free to discuss anything that *they* perceive will threaten this situation. In the case of Shelley and Emily, discussed earlier, both girls were aware that their mother could parent one of them emotionally, but that she had difficulty coping with both. This led to each child being in competition with the other for her position in the family. When her mother was accepting of Shelley, she would fight against anybody whom she perceived as trying to separate her from her mother. This would include denial of the abuse, praise of her mother's position, recognition of how difficult she was to parent and that she deserved to be abused. At times Shelley would not talk to anybody, and stayed silent. It was at these times that she felt most threatened. She needed to resort to silence as she felt unable to control the outcome if she spoke.

When her mother was rejecting of Shelley, and accepting of Emily, Shelley was able to recount her feelings of anger and injustice at her treatment. She had little to lose at this point and could air her feelings. When the mother was rejecting of both girls, they were then emotionally free to support each other and could be affectionate.

Children with conflicting loyalties may find it difficult to say what they want to happen if this involves displeasing one of the parties. This can be seen frequently in families when parents are separating. Children may also experience divided loyalty when asked to say what has happened to them, or what they want to happen, if this is not in their parent's interests.

The importance of key 'signpost' statements

Some messages are difficult for children to convey. They may involve a child compromising her or his potential for healthy attachments or relationships; they may be messages that involve the child overcoming fear before conveying them; or they may contradict what the child perceives is expected. Three examples of 'signpost' statements are discussed below.

1. It is rare for children, as opposed to parents, to make a clear, direct request to speak with a social worker. For some children, this is especially difficult. If they live in a family or community that has a negative view of social services, or if their own life experiences have resulted in difficulties over speaking freely, such a request should be treated seriously and given some priority.
2. Children who state that they do not want to return home may be giving a very strong message. This becomes potentially less significant in adolescence as the struggle for independence comes into play, but caution needs to be taken here as it is sometimes too easy to interpret a teenager's refusal to go home as 'stroppy adolescence', when there could be a valid reason underlying their reluctance. Teenagers with a good relationship with their carer usually still want to live at home; in contrast, a request for time away from home may well be a child's means of trying to resolve a crisis. It is nevertheless a very strong message because separation necessarily means that the child is, at least temporarily, compromising her or his attachment. Care needs to be taken to interpret what is happening for a child to warrant taking such a risk.

An example of both of the above signposts was related to me by an experienced social worker. She explained how she had visited a family regularly for a year because the child, John, had returned home on a Care Order (which eventually was revoked). The worker remained concerned for the child's emotional well-being, believing that he was being scapegoated in the family. She had limited success in engaging the mother but had no success with John, who did not speak to her for a year. Then:

> After one year, John phoned me – after my having seen him regularly and him not talking to me – saying 'Get me out of here, I can't stand it any more' . . . . We talked for two hours – he had had a terrible time.

This worker was able to recognise that the child had become overwhelmed by the maltreatment he had received at home and that he needed an immediate response, which involved removal from his family.

3. Listening to 'survivors' of abuse has informed us of the difficulties that they have in talking about their experiences. Children abused in their family will be compromising their position within it by speaking out; indeed, they may have been threatened in a variety of ways or they may feel that they are to blame. These 'inhibitors to telling' ensure that many victims do not recount their story for some time (if at all). Research has shown consistently that it is much less likely for a retraction of an allegation of sexual abuse to be true than an original allegation. It is important, therefore, to explore in detail what children are saying, their motivation for telling us now and, if they retract, to explore the potential pressures they might have experienced that could have led them to do so.

A case illustration

The following table illustrates how Luke, aged 9, tried to explain his wishes and feelings to a variety of professionals and family members. It can be seen that Luke offered seemingly contradictory messages to some adults, to whom he communicated his immediate needs. When taken out of context of his life as a whole, at first it seemed clear that Luke did not want to return to his mother's care. When his feelings of safety increased, the crisis subsided and he was given more time by the worker. Luke was then able to give a fuller account of his wishes and feelings.

It is significant that, within a meeting that included both the key adults in his life, Luke was unable to say what he needed. It is also clear that he had not yet been able to relinquish responsibility for his future plans to the adults involved.

Situation	Child's statement	To	Factors to take into account
Parent is periodically mentally ill. Luke experiences his mother's schizophrenic episodes			
↓			
Luke goes to live with his grandmother	'I want to stay with you'	Grandmother	• child in crisis • separated from primary attachment figure, needs to secure attachment to grandmother
↓			
Luke's mother goes to his school unannounced to collect him	'I don't want to go with her'	Teacher	• child in crisis • fear of mother's mental illness • not able to predict whether his mother is well
↓			
Mother has contact with Luke, when she recovers from episode of illness	'I want to live with you'	Mother	• need to re-establish primary attachment figure • divided loyalties • is child's perception of decrease in crisis realistic? Can he predict potential for future episodes?
↓			
Social worker 1 sees child	'I want to live with my mum'	Social worker 1	• need to re-establish relationship with primary attachment figure – as above
↓			
Social worker 2 sees child	'I want to be in foster care'	Social worker 2	• child not reassured regarding mother's illness • child anxious
↓			
Social worker 1 sees child again	'I want to live with my mum when she's well'	Social worker 1	• child not in crisis • able to express fear regarding illness • able to express need for mother • able to express need for safety • able to say that he is unable to cope with his mother when she is ill
↓			
Child protection conference	'I haven't decided where I want to live yet'	Meeting	• alien environment • child feeling responsible for the outcome • divided loyalties

Conclusion

Involving children is not just about helping them to attend a meeting or asking them to recount their experiences or their wishes and feelings. It means understanding what they have said, and what they have omitted to say, in the context of their life experiences, their age and development, and their current circumstances. How their story was ascertained and any blocks to the child being able to speak freely need to be identified. Communicating with children and interpreting this is a skilled professional task that needs sensitivity, knowledge and an ability to work with an open mind. Crucially, however, interpreting a child's wishes and feelings – a more complex task than simply ascertaining them – requires professionals to use their judgement.

AUTHORS' CVs

Stewart Betts is a county resources co-ordinator for 'looked after' children in Norfolk Social Services Department.

Marian Brandon is a lecturer in social work and the Director of post-qualifying studies with children and families at the University of East Anglia, Norwich.

Ian Butler is a senior lecturer and research fellow in social work at the University of Wales, Cardiff.

Alison Corner is an independent consultant living in Auckland, New Zealand. Previously she was a training and development manager within social services in Berkshire.

Jim Goddard is a lecturer in social policy at the University of Bradford and has been involved in the Norfolk In-Care Group.

Diana Hinings is a lecturer in social work at the University of East Anglia, Norwich, where she teaches human growth and behaviour.

David Hodgson is a principal lecturer and the Programme Director of undergraduate studies in the School of Social Work at Kingston University.

Professor David Howe is professor of social work at the University of East Anglia, Norwich. He is the editor of *Child and Family Social Work*.

Catherine Kenney is the manager of the Norfolk Guardian ad Litem and Reviewing Officers (GALRO) panel. Previously, she was a senior practitioner in child protection in Norfolk.

Janet Lees is a senior specialist speech and language therapist in the neurodisability service at the Wolfson Centre, Great Ormond Street Hospital for Sick Children and is a lecturer in speech therapy at University College, London.

Dee Lynes has in the past been involved in the Norfolk In-Care Group.

Catherine Rushforth is an independent trainer, consultant and group worker in family support and child protection. She is a qualified social worker and systemic psychotherapist.

Gillian Schofield is a lecturer in psychosocial studies and social work and Deputy Director of the Centre for Research on the child and family at the University of East Anglia, Norwich.

Nicky Scutt is planning and development manager for children and families in Plymouth, Devon, where previously she was area child protection officer.

David Shemmings is a lecturer in social work and the Director of post-qualifying studies in community care at the University of East Anglia, Norwich.

Yvonne Shemmings is an independent consultant and social researcher. Previously she was a service manager (plans and reviews) for 'looked after' children in Essex.

Dr Liz Trinder is a lecturer in social work research at the University of East Anglia, Norwich.

Dr Judith Trowell is a consultant child and adolescent psychiatrist at the Tavistock Clinic, London. She is also the vice-chair of the area child protection committee in Camden, London.

Steve Walker is a training and development manager within social services in Kingston.

Dr Howard Williamson is a senior research associate in the school of social and administrative studies at the University of Wales, Cardiff. He is also the vice-chair of the Wales Youth Agency.

ACKNOWLEDGEMENTS

In addition to expressing my sincere gratitude to each of the authors – especially for their patience – I want to thank Jenny Gray and Ann Gross at the Department of Health for their support and insight.